RISE UP
and
REAP

Letting God's Ideas
Multiply Your Money

Advantage
INSPIRATIONAL

JOHN GREINER

Rise Up And Reap by John Greiner
Copyright © 2006 John Greiner
All Rights Reserved
ISBN: 1-59755-027-2

Published by: *ADVANTAGE BOOKS*™
www.advbooks.com

Unless otherwise indicated, Bible quotations are taken from The Holy Bible, King James Version.

Library of Congress Control Number: 2006928527

First Printing: July 2006
06 07 08 09 10 11 12   9 8 7 6 5 4 3 2 1
Printed in the United States of America

DEDICATION

To Dr. Oral Roberts, a true general in the Body of Christ. Thank you for your faithfulness and excellence of ministry that have impacted me all my Christian life.

In memory of Dr. John Osteen, my spiritual father, for his immeasurable influence in my life. I treasure the years we traveled together to the nations.

ACKNOWLEDGMENTS

This book would not have been written without the help of my wife, Gladys, who so dutifully shared the experiences chronicled here. I also appreciate my son, Jay, and daughter, Claire, who help me enormously.

Thanks also to…

Lee Andrews for your assistance in the manuscript.

Ginny Stinson & Sharon Hester for your help in proofreading.

Dan & Raven Rubottom for introducing me to Dr. Roberts and for your sage advice and input.

Revas Gowan for your encouragement and friendship.

TABLE OF CONTENTS

FOREWORD

You often hear the saying, "Practice what you preach." After nearly 60 years of ministry, I can say that I not only preach the message of Seed-Faith, but I live it. This message has become familiar now, but there is much more to this story than is being told.

Today there is fresh revelation of this principle. It has not been shared with many yet. It is the link between what you are called by God to do and actually accomplishing it. It is a revelation that provides the tools with which we will reap the Great Harvest in these final hours. It is a revelation that has been proven many times over yet has gone unrecognized.

During this latter phase of my ministry, I have opened my home to visits from young preachers who are hungry to hear what God has been saying to me in these final hours.

One such preacher came to me from Houston, Texas. He came to ask more about my vision, *The Wake-Up Call.* But at the end of that interview, he asked what may be one of the most important questions in the Church today: *How will we fund the end-time harvest?*

I'm glad he asked. With a spark in my eye and a smile on my face, I began to share what God had revealed to me regarding *ideas, concepts and insights.* Now this book contains my answer.

Pastor Greiner has expounded on this revelation through extensive research in the Scriptures and has interwoven it with his personal experience regarding the *blessing so abundant there is not room enough to receive.* This is revelation that will change your life, your ministry, and the world.

The message in this book, Rise Up and Reap, is perhaps the most important information you will ever receive regarding God's abundant provision for your own life and for reaping the Great Harvest in this final hour. Jesus is coming soon!

Dr. Oral Roberts

PREFACE

"I'm glad you asked me that question," Dr. Roberts said and smiled.

After I saw Dr. Oral Roberts share his *Wake-Up Call* vision on Christian television, I had the honor of questioning him in person about his visitation from the Lord with a team from my church. Taped in his California home, my interview focused on the cataclysmic wonder of God invading the world—breaking into the life of every man, woman and child with a supernatural sign which Dr. Roberts saw, felt and heard. This Acts 2 sign of blood, fire, and vapor of smoke will trigger the Church's finest hour: the great ingathering of souls into His Kingdom. At what I thought was the end of the interview with this great elder statesman of the faith, I asked a question that has become the beginning of the book you now hold in your hands: *"Since you see such an awesome harvest ahead of us, do you also see a corresponding financial harvest for the Church that tithes and gives?"*

Dr. Roberts' answer poured out with a fresh surge of strength after hours of speaking with me. There had been a second visitation from the Lord just weeks after the first one! The force of the first vision had caused his clothes to flap as he crossed the hallway in his home. He had walked into a divine sonic boom. Now, I was seated near that same hallway and felt something boom in my spirit as he told me of the second *Wake-Up Call*.

What did the Lord say to this man, a veteran of more than 60 years of ministry? **"Wake up!"** He said, "Wake up!" to a Church out of position, in debt, not tithing or tithing incorrectly, and not evangelizing the world. This book is the echo of that sonic boom. God loves us so much that He won't let us sleep through this time of harvest.

At the close of our California interview, one of God's towering champions exhorted me in a commanding voice to preach to my church the whole truth of this second visitation from God. Do it for weeks without fear of people tiring. Do it to get my people to receive their God-ordained, tangible blessings in this life. If they don't receive them, he said, I'm wasting my time and theirs. I accepted the assignment.

A similarly commanding voice had awakened me in the dark, early morning hours of March 1, 1999. It was so harsh that I rebuked it at first as if it were from satan, thinking I could roll over and go back to sleep. Finally, I recognized my Father calling me and my generation to attention. "Wake up the Church," He said. I jumped to attention by my bedside. "They're like you. They're asleep in their beds, and when I speak to them, they think it's the devil."

Worldwide evangelism takes money—lots of it. Yes, inheriting our blessings allows us to take our place in funding His work, but it serves another divine purpose:

we're to be signposts of His glory in this dark world. Here is revelation to shake us awake to the financial side of the signs of His coming. The Lord of the Harvest is positioning you and me to leave nothing on the table as we reap and gather for His Kingdom.

John Greiner

INTRODUCTION

Hold on Just a Minute There, Lord!

Will a man rob God? Yet ye have robbed me. But ye say, Wherein have we robbed thee? In tithes and offerings. Ye are cursed with a curse: for ye have robbed me, even this whole nation.

Bring ye all the tithes into the storehouse, that there may be meat in mine house, and prove me now herewith, saith the Lord of hosts, if I will not open you the windows of heaven, and pour you out a blessing, that there shall not be room enough to receive it. And I will rebuke the devourer for your sakes, and he shall not destroy the fruits of your ground; neither shall your vine cast her fruit before the time in the field, saith the Lord of hosts. And all nations shall call you blessed: for ye shall be a delightsome land, saith the Lord of hosts.
-Malachi 3:8-12

My people are out of position for the end-time harvest, in deep credit card debt, tithing incorrectly or not tithing at all, and not evangelizing the world. Even if I told them to go and take off two weeks and travel to share the gospel, they cannot go because of payments. Their debt level is so high. The credit system of this world has just bound them. They are unable to do what they want to do because of this horrible debt situation. Many and most don't tithe. -Dr. Oral Roberts

These were some of the Lord's words to describe the financial state of His Church. Sounding like a financial State of the Union address, His words to Dr. Roberts painted a picture of so many Christians barely making it from paycheck to paycheck. Indeed, a 2005 study conducted by the Barna Group[1] revealed that only nine percent of born-again adults had actually tithed the previous year.

What is lacking in the wallets of the generation called to reap a supernatural harvest out of this natural world? More importantly, what solution did the Lord offer to Dr. Roberts? *"Tell My people to bring the whole tithe into the storehouse,"* the Lord began. But before He got to the part of that familiar scripture regarding the *"blessing that there shall not be room enough to receive,"* Dr. Roberts stopped Him: "Hold on just a minute there, Lord. I've been a tither for more than 50 years, and I have never been in that condition when I couldn't hold the blessing. In fact, I don't know anybody who *has* been in that condition."

I appreciate the candor of such a great general of the faith. There I was, sitting in the home of a well-known

Christian leader, but I could have been in your home or mine or that of any other faithful tither. None of us has ever been in the position of saying, "God, hold the money back; I have too much to handle."

Dr. Roberts asked the same question you or I would ask. He asked the question many believers have asked while seated at their kitchen tables in tears. They're trying to figure out how to pay their bills, yet they go ahead and write out their tithe checks first. Who hasn't ever looked at their remaining 90 percent and known it wasn't enough for the month? Who hasn't ever looked at lack and said, "Where's the promise, Lord?" God's people of faith don't dwell on their questions. Most just keep on obeying God: tithing and giving offerings over and above the tithe. They're doing the right things, yet many aren't getting the right results. Why?

I've been at that kitchen table with my own checkbook. As a faithful tither, I've suffered land foreclosure, houses that wouldn't sell, and ruinous losses in business. Of course, I have also received great blessings to a measure. There has been a measure of blessing for all tithers, but as Dr. Roberts stated, not to the extent that it cannot be held.

The way we have functioned in tithing and giving is to plant the seed and expect God to drop the blessings right on our heads. "If I give money, I'll get money back. If I tithe, I receive the return in money." But in thinking like that, we leave out one important step.

Imagine a farmer planting a crop, then just taking a seat and saying, "Now, I'm going to get a crop." Where I grew up in the grain fields of south Texas, you couldn't just plant the grain and leave it at that. You had to have a harvesting instrument, like a combine harvester, to go through the fields efficiently working to actually reap the harvest.

According to the word God spoke to Dr. Roberts, *ideas* are our combine harvesters. They contain the instruments we have needed to reap the harvest from our tithes. I believe God is pouring out those profitable *ideas, concepts and insights* on His people today, and they're coming at exactly the right time for maximum benefit to us and to His Kingdom.

John Greiner, Pastor
Glorious Way Church
Houston, Texas

Chapter One

Ideas, Concepts and Insights

Will a man rob God? Yet ye have robbed Me. But ye say, Wherein have we robbed thee? In tithes and offerings. Ye are cursed with a curse: for ye have robbed me, even this whole nation.

Bring ye all the tithes into the storehouse, that there may be meat in mine house, and prove me now herewith, saith the Lord of hosts, if I will not open you the windows of heaven, and pour you out a blessing, that there shall not be room enough to receive it. And I will rebuke the devourer for your sakes, and he shall not destroy the fruits of your ground; neither shall your vine cast her fruit before the time in the field, saith the Lord of hosts. And all nations shall call you blessed: for ye shall be a delightsome land, saith the Lord of hosts. - Malachi 3:8-12

Change Your Expectations

God wants to wake up every tither and get us looking in the right direction for the harvest. No matter how faithfully or consistently you have brought your tithe into the storehouse of your local church, tithing with the wrong expectations will never produce the abundance needed to reap the end-time harvest. For your tithe to produce more than you can contain, you will need to align your expectations with God's purposes when you bring your tithe to Him. Bring it also with a love for God and a burning desire to see the gospel preached all over the world. Then you will not be laboring to grow rich in this life, but you will be laboring to please God. Your labor will be one of faith— faith to receive what He has freely given. It doesn't have to be hard.

Malachi 3 tells us that if we'll tithe, God will open up the windows of heaven and pour us out a blessing that there shall not be room enough to receive. We have visions of material things falling from the sky like ripe cherries off of a tree and piling up all around us. After all, we know that all riches belong to God, but it seems His storehouse of material wealth resides on earth, not in heaven:

The earth is the Lord's, and the fulness thereof; the world, and they that dwell therein. -Psalm 24:1

For every beast of the forest is mine, and the cattle upon a thousand hills. -Psalm 50:10

If everything we need is already on the *earth*, then what does God pour out from *heaven*? Dr. Roberts' revelation from God answered the question in the heart of every tither:

*You are looking at me, and while it is true that I am your source, I cannot directly give you the money, cars, houses and whatever else you need. Everything that you need is on the earth. It is not up here. When I open the windows and pour out, I don't pour out cars, money or houses. What I pour out are **ideas, concepts and insights.** I will bring so many ideas that you finally say, "Lord, no more ideas, please. I can't take it."* - Dr. Oral Roberts

God knows where the wealth of this world lies, and He will show it to His people as they look to Him. Some ideas from God about both making and saving money can multiply your finances, while others can reach past the material world to affect every aspect of your life. With the right expectations, you will operate in this world's economy masterfully, reaping its benefits by trading, by wisdom, and by ideas poured out on the tither from heaven's open windows. Are you willing to make adjustments for abundance?

One Idea Can Change Everything

Dr. Roberts used Henry Ford's Model T as an example of an idea poured out by God. In 1915, an automobile cost between $3000 and $5000, roughly an entire year's salary for the average man. As a result, only a rich man could afford an automobile. So Henry Ford began to ask, "How can I produce an automobile everyone can afford?"

His idea would revolutionize the world: the assembly line. Now workers could specialize in their tasks so that each one completed a small part of each vehicle as it traveled down the line. In the most efficient way possible, the Model T was mass produced, and at the end of the line, it had a "sticker price" of just $500.

The birth of this one idea instantly changed the way America manufactured goods. The Industrial Revolution began, and we transformed from a horse-and-buggy economy into a mobile, motorized society. Farmers got out from behind mules, hopped on tractors and "sped" away—increasing productivity and wealth for themselves, the nation, and eventually the world.

Ideas Are Poured Out by God

Ideas like the Ford assembly line are poured out of heaven by God. As tithers, shouldn't we believe for them and receive them in greater measure than those who don't tithe? The Old and the New Testaments are full of examples that verify Dr. Roberts' word from the Lord about heavenly ideas. One of the most powerful examples is the Genesis 28 story of how Jacob became rich.

Here we plainly see heaven's ideas received and redounding to the account of a man who obeyed God in tithing. Jacob, whose name means *supplanter* or *deceiver*, was a momma's boy who fooled his daddy, stole his elder brother's inheritance, and had to run for his life. But on the way, he had a visitation from God that changed his life. During that divine encounter, he made a vow to tithe and give God the first tenth:

> *And Jacob vowed a vow, saying, If God will be with me, and will keep me in this way that I go, and will give me bread to eat, and raiment to put on, So that I come again to my father's house in peace; then shall the Lord be my God: And this stone, which I have set for a pillar, shall be God's house: and of all that thou shalt give me I will surely give the tenth unto thee.*
> *-Genesis 28:20-22*

After going to his uncle Laban's sheep ranch and working 14 years for the hands in marriage of Laban's two daughters, Jacob asked to leave. But his new father-in-law didn't want to let him go.

> *...I pray thee, if I have found favor is thine eyes, tarry: for I have learned by experience that the Lord hath blessed me for thy sake.... Appoint me thy wages and I will give it.*
> *-Genesis 30:27-28*

Jacob's response is a biblical example of an idea poured out by God to a tither. Like Henry Ford's Model T, this idea also increased a farmer's productivity exponentially and revolutionized his world. Jacob and others from the Bible not only confirm God's words in the *Wake-Up Call* visitation, but they build our faith that ideas from God are every tither's right. God gave Jacob this idea because he was a tither.

> *And he (Laban) said, What shall I give thee?
> And Jacob said, Thou shalt not give me
> anything: if thou will do this thing for me, I will
> again feed and keep thy flock. I will pass
> through all thy flock today, removing from
> thence all the speckled and spotted cattle, and
> all the brown cattle among the sheep, and the
> spotted and speckled among the goats: and of
> such shall be my hire. -Genesis 30:31-32*

Jacob basically said that he didn't want Laban to *give* him anything. Instead, he would *take* all the inferior spotted and speckled ones out of Laban's herd and raise them three days' journey away (Genesis 30:36). Where did he get that idea? Taking the inferior ones is an idea poured out from God that certainly did not come from human reasoning or Jacob's genius-level intellect. As you'll see, it was Jacob's "inferior" livestock that eventually grew to be superior in strength and number to those of Laban.

Ideas Are the Tither's Right

God wants to pour out ideas to everyone who tithes, and He even said, "Prove me!" You can be confident that His Word is true, and it does work. If you bring the *whole tithe* in the storehouse, God is going to give *you* a lucrative idea. There are so many ways for people to make money. Some of them are so simple that you see them and think, "Why didn't I think of that?" Like Jacob, you can have an idea from God that can make you rich.

Tithing releases wisdom. With the wisdom of God's ideas, you'll know what to do and when to do it in order to increase and not suffer loss. Some ideas are as simple as a way to save money, and saving money is just like making money. Others are creative ideas for complex strategies that can change the world. You have a Bible right to access the ideas of God. His ideas make tremendous breakthrough available in your life and finances, but first you must be faithful over the small things. God often leads us in small stages. For example, start with doing what you can to get out of debt, so that you'll have freedom to pursue the next stage. Change your thinking. This is His work. This is His plan.

The devil will try to get you to say, "No, getting ideas from God is for Brother So-and-So because he is better qualified than I am. I didn't go to college. I didn't have this or that advantage in life." God is not trying to turn every tither into a rocket scientist or an engineer. You don't have be a computer wizard, a genius or an inventor with a wild, pie-in-the-sky idea. God will often give simple ideas in a field of expertise that you already have. Jacob knew livestock, so his ideas for wealth involved livestock. Henry Ford knew automobiles. Everyone knows *something*. What do you know?

Some of you are under such intense financial pressure that you feel disqualified from getting God's ideas. Maybe you're burdened by heavy debt. For others, it may be feelings of hopelessness or victimization over past mistakes. "Why would God give *me* any ideas?" We must resist the urge to reject any fresh truth about tithing just because of discouragement; we have faithfully tithed for so long without abundant reaping that we have to renew our expectation for increase.

In my own Christian life prior to my pastoral ministry, I made my living as a custom homebuilder and attended a large Houston church. My pastor preached 37 consecutive messages on tithing at a season in my life when I was struggling financially. I could hardly pay my bills. I was a tither. I believed in tithing, but I didn't want to hear anything about the benefits because I wasn't reaping them. Listening to those 37 messages was almost an assault on my faith as I heard about all the blessings, yet didn't see any of them coming my way! In my case, I had been out of the will of God in my business. It took time for God to reposition me for His blessing. Don't allow your way of thinking to disqualify you from your wealthy future.

> *For ye know the grace of our Lord Jesus Christ, that, though he was rich, yet for your sakes he became poor, that ye through his poverty might be rich. -II Corinthians 8:9*

"Might" means that we have a choice. We've all missed ideas or wasted divine opportunities or connections at one time or another. Part of the freshness of the *Wake-Up Call* revelation is that God is giving the Church a new start to bring our financial health in line with the demands of the harvest. Jesus is coming soon, and the funding of the gospel can't wait. Turn 180 degrees from victimization. Repent for past mistakes, and go forward. Making you the head and not the tail was God's idea from the very beginning. Satan wants you to agree with him that you're disqualified, but God is not a liar. He made you to be the top.

Jacob started out poor; he had to work to get his wife. But he was *willing* to become rich. It's God's will for you to be rich, also. You might say, "Rich? Why do I need to be *rich*? I don't need that much. I lead a simple life." Fine. Get rich; keep your lifestyle just like it is, and give the rest to missions. Send people to the nations.

Your Brain Versus God's

And Jacob took him rods of green poplar, and of the hazel and chestnut tree; and pilled white strakes in them, and made the white appear which was in the rods. And he set the rods which he had pilled before the flocks in the gutters in the watering troughs when the flocks came to drink, that they should conceive when they came to drink. And the flocks conceived before the rods, and brought forth cattle ringstraked, speckled, and spotted.

And Jacob did separate the lambs, and set the faces of the flocks toward the ringstraked, and all the brown in the flock of Laban; and he put his own flocks by themselves, and put them not unto Laban's cattle. And it came to pass, whensoever the stronger cattle did conceive, that Jacob laid the rods before the eyes of the cattle in the gutters, that they might conceive among the rods. But when the cattle were feeble, he put them not in: so the feebler were Laban's, and the stronger Jacob's. And the man increased exceedingly, and had much cattle, and maidservants, and menservants, and camels, and asses.
-Genesis 30:37-43

"Whittle sticks, and stick them in the mud over there by the feeding trough at mating season" were basically God's first instructions. The Lord told Jacob that when the animals mated, they would bring forth speckled, spotted and brown cattle. Who ever heard of that? Jacob apparently did not have a degree in Animal Science from Texas A&M University. How can looking at a spotted stick while mating produce livestock with spots? It wouldn't have worked except that it was a supernatural idea from God. Of course, God can give you natural ideas, but He

> *God doesn't drop ideas into the mind of the tither.*
> *He drops them into your spirit.*
> ⌘

can also give you supernatural ideas that will bring a harvest out of this natural world.

The breeding and multiplication of cattle is not supernatural. It is a natural process that involves mating, but God's idea about the sticks made the difference. Jacob, like Henry Ford (and perhaps like you one day), became rich from one idea. Here, he became rich out of that one idea and a series of *concepts* that God gave him with the idea. Wisdom, insight and revelations from God made him rich. He was so wealthy, in fact, that he had to divide his group into two bands on the way back to see his brother, Esau (Genesis 32).

Jacob did not come up with the spotted stick idea by having a long brainstorming session with his two wives, concubines, daughter, and 12 sons. They didn't get together and toss some ideas around about moving to California, being discovered as the next acting talent, and making a fortune. The idea was not dropped into the brain of one of Jacob's family members. God doesn't drop ideas into the *mind* of the tither; He drops them into your *spirit.* Then, as you pray in tongues, the ideas will come up into your mind. God is a Spirit and He speaks to us Spirit-to-spirit. He does not deal with your mind; He deals with your spirit.

For he that speaketh in an unknown tongue speaketh not unto men, but unto God: for no man understandeth him; howbeit in the spirit he speaketh mysteries. -I Corinthians 14:2

Even though Nashville or Motown may have brainstorming sessions to try to write new songs, if an idea does not come by revelation in your spirit, then it is just flesh. Stay full of the Holy Ghost and pray in tongues. Then God's poured-out ideas will bubble up, and all of sudden, you will become aware of what you should do. Sometimes you won't understand why, but you'll become aware of the right ideas.

Prayer Uncovers God's Ideas

There is hidden wisdom God has for each of us who tithe. It will move from your spirit into your conscious awareness if you pray in the Spirit.

> **But we speak the wisdom of God in a mystery, even the hidden wisdom, which God ordained before the world unto our glory.**
> **-I Corinthians 2:7**

The Father has these ideas that He has hidden before the foundations of the world, whether it is the spotted stick that unlocked Jacob's wealth or the Model T assembly line for Henry Ford. They are hidden *"unto our glory,"* meaning He has held them back and kept them for you and me.

So why don't we have these ideas? We haven't prayed for them. We haven't believed for them. We haven't waited on God for them. We've been stressed out working three jobs, shuttling the kids around, trying to maintain a four bedroom house and a lifestyle that takes all of our energy and all of our time. It is difficult to receive an idea from God without getting over into the Holy Ghost and enlisting the help of the Helper.

Another hindrance to praying for God's ideas is our casual attitude about being led by the Spirit. Just having the presence of God with us as Christians doesn't guarantee the thumbs-up of God's approval to any fleshly idea or approach we devise. If God did not author it, it will not succeed. Wouldn't you rather have an idea rain down through the open windows of heaven and bubble up into your spirit?

> *Blessed is the man that walketh not in the counsel of the ungodly, nor standeth in the way of sinners, nor sitteth in the seat of the scornful. But his delight is in the law of the Lord; and in his law doth he meditate day and night. And he shall be like a tree planted by the rivers of water, that bringeth forth his fruit in his season; his leaf also shall not wither; and whatsoever he doeth shall prosper. -Psalm 1:1-3*

Notice that the final promise of prosperity is directed toward the man who not only avoids the pitfalls of verse 1, but also delights in the law of the Lord and meditates on it constantly. Staying in the Spirit and allowing our roots to drink continually from Holy Spirit rivers ensures that our ideas have God's breath of life in them. Then we can expect those ideas to prosper.

Ideas, Your Resource

What would have happened if Jacob had just blindly carried on at Laban's ranch and said, "Lord, You know that I'm a tither. I'm expecting Laban to bless me as I keep on faithfully working for him for another 14 years"? Probably nothing much. Jacob's job was not his source.

Some of us have been wrongly expecting the tithe to produce a kind of automatic benefit for us. We tithe and immediately expect the boss to bless us, as if a raise or bonus will be the return benefit of our tithe. The blessings and benefits of the tithe are not automatic. They require us to be alert and active. God rains down ideas, but we have been staying out of the rain to wait for what is tangible. We think that the tithe will come back as money—maybe a raise on the job or an inheritance check in the mail.

Your job is not your source. How many times have we made that statement and not really meant it? Too often we continue treating our jobs as our sole supply. In reality, your job is just a vehicle of provision so that you will have seed to sow.

> *...but rather let him labour, working with his hands that thing which is good, that he may have to give to him that needeth. -Ephesians 4:28*

Working your job allows you to give to those who don't have. Even though promotions, raises and bonuses occasionally occur on your job and bring a measure of increase, God's ideas will bring you from mere provision, to a place of abundance, and finally to *"exceeding abundantly above all that you can ask or think"* (Ephesians 3:20).

What if you hate your job? Some of you do hate it. Just humble yourself. It is a job. Your job is a place for you to have seed to sow and sustain you while you wait for ideas to come to fruition. Your job is not your living. Ideas are your living, and you'll soon need to work at your new livelihood of bringing ideas to fruition.

> *Your job is not your living.*
>
> *Ideas are your living.*
>
> ⌘

Praying out the plan of God for the idea He gave you is part of that work. You can't sit around and wait for things to happen. Do some research. Investigate ways to execute your idea from God, and if you hit a dead end, simply begin in a new direction. Whatever you're paying attention to in life, that is the direction you are going to be headed. If you pay a great amount of attention to vacationing, TV, movies or recreation, you will probably never be rich. You will be a consumer. Always spending more than you should, your life will be about consuming goods. But if you pray a lot, get ideas from heaven, and work on them as He leads, you will be a distributor for the Kingdom of God in these last days.

God Saved the Best Ideas for Last

...Every man at the beginning doth set forth good wine; and when men have well drunk,

then that which is worse: but thou hast kept the good wine until now. -John 2:10

I believe one reason God has saved the best until last is to keep us from getting off course and from squandering end-time fortunes before the harvest was ready. The great ingathering of souls will require billions worldwide. An influx of billions of dollars would tempt some of us to trust God less and depend on ourselves more. The larger the budget, the more we must guard against trusting in the money. It's very easy when the accounts are fat to assume that God is pleased with every expenditure, when in reality, presumption has entered into the equation. God wants us to be dependent on His Holy Spirit no matter the size of the budget.

As we are living in the last of the last days, God is bringing greater ideas with greater frequency. Never has there been such opportunity. When you're a tither, God is faithful to bring you a harvest where you have labored. Ideas that can make you rich are part of that harvest. Dr. Roberts said the Lord told him, *"My people are cheating themselves."* How? By not tithing or by tithing with the wrong expectations.

Expect the best ideas to pour on you from heaven's windows when you tithe. For example, one tithing businessman in my church got the idea to sell his oil-field related business worth several million dollars. God provided a buyer at a price that greatly blessed him, and his tithe greatly blessed the church. The buyer, though, was not so blessed. One year later he had to declare bankruptcy. The tithing businessman had sold at the peak of the oil price, getting top dollar for the business. If he had waited, the consequences would have been disastrous. God's ideas are always supernatural and right on time.

Jacob's spotted stick was a poured-out idea that God sent because he was a tither. It was a pretty simple idea. Sometimes we hold out for some grandiose idea that will make us instant billionaires, and we miss God's simple idea because we are not paying attention. But Jacob paid attention, obeyed, and started whittling.

> ***And Jacob took him rods of green poplar, and of the hazel and chestnut tree; and pilled white strakes in them, and made the white appear which was in the rods. -Genesis 30:37***

He took some limbs from three different kinds of trees—green poplar, hazel and chestnut—and stripped off the bark to make them appear speckled. Who in the world would think these sticks would do anything? The steps and instructions God gave him about the stick were totally supernatural.

> ***And he set the rods which he had pilled before the flocks in the gutters in the watering troughs when the flocks came to drink, that they should conceive when they came to drink.***
> ***-Genesis 30:38***

The idea is so supernatural that it could appear foolish but the foolishness of God is wiser than men.

> ***Because the foolishness of God is wiser than men…. But God hath chosen the foolish things***

*of the world to confound the wise; and God
hath chosen the weak things of the world to
confound the things which are mighty....
-I Corinthians 1:25, 27*

Through the foolishness of a stick (God's poured-out idea), Jacob successfully produced spotted cattle.

*And the flocks conceived before the rods, and
brought forth cattle ringstraked, speckled, and
spotted. -Genesis 30:39*

After Jacob proved to God that he would be faithful to develop the poured-out idea and turn it into a concept, he received another idea.

*And Jacob did separate the lambs, and set the
faces of the flocks toward the ringstraked, and
all the brown in the flock of Laban; and he put
his own flocks by themselves, and put them not
unto Laban'cattle.*

*And it came to pass, whensoever the stronger
cattle did conceive, that Jacob laid the rods
before the eyes of the cattle in the gutters, that
they might conceive among the rods. But when
the cattle were feeble, he put them not in: so the
feebler were Laban's, and the stronger Jacob's.
-Genesis 30:40-42*

His idea of separating the weaker ones and letting them mate with Laban's cattle and not his own may have been judgment from God for Laban's deceit over Rachel, or it may just have been Jacob's flesh retaliating. Either way, eventually Laban's cattle got weaker, and Jacob's became stronger and more plentiful until at the end, he had a great herd. As Jacob developed his simple *idea*, it became a *concept* which had greater impact. He kept working on his idea until he got *insight* from heaven to develop it into more of a blessing. Jacob made the progression from an idea to a concept with the birth of the spotted cattle, but how long and how much work did it take? The answer may lie in Dr. Roberts' words to us:

> *Once you have an idea, then you have to investigate it and study it out. You have to pray over it, start working and developing it into a concept, into a way of life. Once you're actually executing that idea, God will give you insight, or wisdom, as to how to operate.*

God will help you to maneuver and navigate your way toward bringing the idea to fruition and causing it to make you rich. He will give you wisdom and revelation about the situation, but you cannot just snap your fingers. Perhaps you'll have to consult with people who know something about what God is talking to you about, or you may have to do some research at the library or on the internet. It is going to take work to put your idea into action. God pours out ideas for you, but He expects you, like Jacob, to get them off the ground. When you are faithful to act on *His* ideas and turn them into concepts, He gives you insight, or wisdom, to prosper.

Be a Faithful Steward of God's Idea

Moreover it is required in stewards, that a man be found faithful. -I Corinthians 4:2

We must prove ourselves to be good stewards because God won't increase someone who is not wisely handling what he has already been given. For some of us that will mean proving to God that we have changed our way of doing things.

You will have to crucify the flesh and be led by the Spirit—not just in prayer or in spiritual things like getting people saved or laying hands on the sick—but you must also prove you are led by the Spirit concerning money. Elevate your sense of responsibility. You're not just a servant, but a *son and heir* of the Most High God.

And unto one he gave five talents, to another two, and to another one; to every man according to his several ability....
-Matthew 25:15

A "talent" is a form of currency, a piece of money. God gave one man five, one man two, and the third man one. The guy with five went out and traded and said, "Here, Lord. Your five has gained five more." The guy with two went out and traded and said, "Here, Lord. Your two has gained two more." Notice it was all God's: "*Your* five, Lord," and

"*Your* two, Lord." Everything you have belongs to Him. Every idea began with Him.

The Father originates, Jesus administrates, and the Holy Spirit demonstrates the idea. Ideas originate with the Father. He gives them to Jesus, who is the administrator or Head of the Church. Jesus administrates the distribution of these ideas to believers individually according to their ability, their faithfulness and according to whatever His wisdom is for the life and destiny of that individual. Each believer also has the Holy Ghost who is the demonstrator. Jesus said, "The Holy Ghost will take of mine and reveal it to you."

> ***...for he (the Spirit of Truth) shall receive of mine, and shall shew it unto you. -John 16:14***

The guy who had one talent wrapped it up in a napkin and hid it in the backyard. He was afraid of losing it, so he did nothing. God gives us ideas, and He wants us to do something with them. An idea becomes a concept when it becomes a way of life.

John Greiner

Chapter Two

Old Testament Ingenuity

Let's look at four Old Testament tithers—Isaac, Abraham, Joseph, and Joshua—who received ideas that revolutionized their worlds. The paths they took from ideas to concepts to insight will give us more light in which to work before night comes and the door shuts on the great ingathering of souls. We need every key the Bible offers to break open the treasure of the *Wake-Up Call* revelation and get God's harvest out of this world.

First, let me establish that these fathers of the faith were tithers. We know that Isaac tithed because the only way for a man to approach God was over a bleeding sacrifice. From the time of Adam, the blood has served to cleanse and give men an approach to God. When Adam and Eve sinned and became aware of their nakedness after losing their glory covering, God gave them the skin of animals He had killed. Abel, a tither, also knew that shed blood was required in order to approach God, and the only acceptable sacrifice was the offering of an unblemished firstborn male, the first fruits of your herds. Since Isaac was obviously in right standing with God and received His promise, he had to be a tither.

The Bible tells us that Abraham tithed to Melchizedek:

> *And Melchizedek king of Salem brought forth bread and wine: and he was the priest of the most high God. And he blessed him, and said, Blessed be Abram of the most high God, possessor of heaven and earth: And blessed be the most high God, which hath delivered thine enemies into thy hand. And he gave him tithes of all. –Genesis 14:18-20*

Certainly, Abraham would have passed on tithing to his son Isaac who would have taught his son Jacob. We have proof that Jacob tithed in Genesis 28:22:

> *"And this stone, which I (Jacob) have set for a pillar, shall be God's house: and of all that thou shalt give me I will surely give the tenth unto thee."*

As for Joseph, we can probably assume his father, Jacob, taught him to tithe. The Bible does teach us that Joseph was a good steward of money entrusted to him. Though he had no income to tithe while in prison, can we agree that if he had had any income, he would have tithed? And of Joshua, the Bible says he was a man of the whole Word. He observed to do all that was written therein (Joshua 1:8); therefore, he was a tither.

The Fight of Faith

These four men all had to contend for what God gave them. Will you have to contend? Yes! Will you have to fight the good fight of faith? Yes! Is everything immediately going to be rosy peachy-keen? No! There is no single instant-rich, instant-debt-free scripture for you to confess every day. God pours out ideas for tithers who are believing to receive them, but you will have to contend for those ideas to come to fruition.

You'll also become an even bigger target for the devil when God's ideas begin to come to you. The enemy attacks with fury those of us who believe this way, and he will try to talk you out of any idea from heaven. Once the idea comes forth and you begin to execute the concept, you will have to use your authority as a believer to beat the devil's brains out to possess your land. Don't faint and don't back up.

Isaac's Idea: Sowing in Famine

> *And there was a famine in the land…. Then Isaac sowed in that land, and in the same year received an hundredfold; and the Lord blessed him. -Genesis 26:1, 12*

In Genesis 26, we read of Isaac who went to Gerar (present day Gaza), planted seed, and in the same year, received a hundredfold. He did something that made no sense in the natural: he planted a crop in the middle of a dust bowl. I have preached Isaac's story more times then I can count, but until I heard Dr. Roberts, I had never tied it to the *idea* of sowing in a famine. Who would plant a crop in a dust bowl unless God told them to do it? It was a supernatural idea, and it demonstrated that the believing tither is not tied to the weather. We are not tied to the depression or other fluctuations of the economy in which we live. We give too much credence to the economic climate of this nation. In actuality, we are independent of this economy. Many of us say this, but we haven't really believed it. God wants us to come up higher.

Where did this idea to sow in a famine come from? It wasn't just a wild decision Isaac made one afternoon, "You know what? I think I'll buy a bunch of seed and sow it out there in that dirt in this famine." The Holy Ghost had told him, "I'm going to bless you in that land."

> *And the Lord appeared unto him, and said....*
> *Sojourn in this land, and I will be with thee,*
> *and will bless thee.... -Genesis 26:2-3*

Even before Isaac received the supernatural poured-out idea, he had already been divinely directed to go to this land and was promised that he would be blessed when he got there. Because of his obedience to go and his faith, he received a hundredfold the same year.

I have preached frequently on the hundredfold, and I have received more than a hundredfold a time or two, but not consistently. If we received it consistently, churches would have enough to build new facilities without borrowing money. Church buildings are barns for the harvest. I know the lost people of the world are going to come into the Church and bring their wealth, but we should not wait on that. God wants to bless His people now. He said, "*My people are cheating themselves,*" and He is giving us the information we need to repent, change and increase.

> **And the man (Isaac) waxed great, and went forward, and grew until he became very great: For he had possession of flocks and possession of herds, and great store of servants: and the Philistines envied him. -Genesis 26:13-14**

These verses of scripture refer to *financial* greatness and wealth, not *spiritual* greatness. Like Isaac, we will be envied by this world as God's blessing overtakes us. Many of us are awake and aware that Jesus is coming soon, but He wants us *all* awake and in position financially for His end-time plans and purposes.

Maintain Divine Supply Lines

Isaac, the Jewish man living in the midst of the Philistines, became very great financially, was greatly envied, and lived happily ever after, right? No! A fight began about water.

> **And Isaac digged again the wells of water, which they had digged in the days of Abraham his father; for the Philistines had stopped them after the death of Abraham.... And the herdmen of Gerar did strive with Isaac's herdmen saying, The water is ours....**

*And they digged another well, and strove for
that also.... -Genesis 26:18, 20-21*

A most important lesson can be gleaned from Isaac's
battle to flourish while surrounded by the enemy: maintain
divine supply lines. Water is a type of the Holy Ghost.
After the ideas begin to flow and God prospers you, make
sure you maintain a proper and adequate supply of the Holy
Ghost.

I have seen a lot of people whom God has blessed begin
to think it is all due to the fact they are such sharp
businessmen, such good negotiators and so swift in their
thinking. They quit praying. Sometimes they start stealing a
little of the tithe. "Well, it is so much money. I can't afford
to tithe that much money." Perhaps they need prayer to
make less money so there'd be less to tithe! I have seen it. I
watched their heads swell as they forgot that God gave them
the idea, gave them a business, and made them the boss.
Remember, no matter how many cattle, employees, oil wells,
car dealerships, or daycare centers you may have, you're still
going to need a steady supply of fresh ideas from the Holy
Ghost to maintain them. No enterprise can survive without
His living water, but the devil will always try to strangle
God's supply.

A Grain of Sense before a Grain of Sand

No small vision, God's plan for the children of Israel was always about millions and multitudes. He revealed to Abraham:

> ***That in blessing I will bless thee, and in multiplying I will multiply thy seed as the stars of heaven, and as the sand which is upon the sea shore; and thy seed shall possess the gate of his enemies.... -Genesis 22:17***

Even so, it involved small beginnings and easy stages. Sometimes we are praying for something really big, but we don't have the capacity to take care of what we're praying to receive. We need to stay within the limits of our faith and let God bless us in easy stages.

God didn't bring the children of Israel into the Promised Land until they had multiplied to millions of people. They were just seventy at first, which is why He took them to Egypt so they could grow. They could not possibly possess the land in those few numbers.

> *Maintain a consistent prayer life so you will hear the ideas you need from God.*
>
> ⌘

John Greiner

As a tither you have a financial Promised Land, but like Isaac and Abraham, you will have to start moving towards it in basic, baby steps of faithfulness and consistency. You have to walk before you can run. You have to crawl before you can walk. You have to be able to roll and turn over before you can even crawl. God is very practical. You will need a support system before you can move into multiplied millions as the grains of sand. We can see this in the life of Abraham in Genesis 13:

> *And Abram was very rich in cattle, in silver and in gold…. And Lot also, which went with Abram, had flocks, and herds, and tents. And the land was not able to bear them….*
> *-Genesis 13:2, 5-6*

The land was not able to bear them because there was neither enough water nor enough pasture for both of them. There was not enough room, and all of a sudden, Abraham got an idea from God: "Lot, you choose."

> *Is not the whole land before thee? Separate thyself, I pray thee, from me: if thou wilt take the left hand, then I will go to the right; or if thou depart to the right hand, then I will go to the left. -Genesis 13:9*

48

What Would You Choose?

Lot chose the land of Sodom and Gomorrah. "I'm tired of tent living. I'm more of an urban person. Never mind that this is a wicked city, I am going to get involved."

> *And Lot lifted up his eyes, and beheld all the plain of Jordan, that it was well watered every where, before the Lord destroyed Sodom and Gomorrah, even as the garden of the Lord.... Then Lot chose him all the plain of Jordan.... But the men of Sodom were wicked and sinners before the Lord exceedingly. -Genesis 13:10-11, 13*

Lot didn't lay on his face and say, "Lord, what should I do?" He didn't pray. He chose a carnal idea. Lot was willing to compromise and base his choice on what he could see, taste, touch, smell, and hear—on his five senses. He compromised on the basis of appearances, and it almost cost him everything. A lack of prayer means there will be a lack of poured-out ideas from God. There will be no godly concept to develop and no insight, or wisdom, as to the direction we should go in life.

What did Abraham get for choosing God's idea?

> *And the Lord said unto Abram, after that Lot was separated from him, Lift up now thine eyes, and look from the place where thou art northward, and southward, and eastward, and westward: For all the land*

*which thou seest, to thee will I give it, and
to thy seed for ever. -Genesis 13:14-15*

"I'm going to give it all to you, boy," was what God said
to him. Equally important as the land was the idea God gave
him that "anywhere I go, I will be blessed." Abraham took
this poured-out idea from God and developed it into a
concept or lifestyle. We can track that idea throughout the
lives of this man and his seed and see that it became insight
and wisdom to them.

Abraham's faith was so activated in the idea of God's
blessing that he didn't worry about the circumstances. He
knew he could get blessed anywhere because he was
following God. Let the stock market go up or down. Cattle
futures can take a hit. God sees upcoming fluctuations, and
He can always give you an idea that will put you on top. He
can tell you to pull your money out of one place and invest it
somewhere else. Like Abraham, get your faith so activated
in God's blessing for the tither who is believing Him for
ideas, concepts and insights that you take your eyes off the
circumstances. Let God choose your pathway. Then, as the
blessings come, keep your eyes on the source.

The Eye Test

*And they took Lot, Abram's brother's son, who
dwelt in Sodom, and his goods, and departed....
And when Abram heard that his brother was
taken captive, he armed his trained servants,
born in his own house, three hundred and
eighteen, and pursued them unto Dan. And he*

divided himself against them... and smote them, and pursued them.... And he brought back all the goods, and also brought again his brother Lot, and his goods, and the women also, and the people. -Genesis 14:12, 14-16

Abraham's eye was always on the source of his blessing, never on the circumstances or the stuff. After the rescue of his nephew, Lot, a reward was offered to Abraham by the King of Sodom. Abraham declined with these words:

...I have lift up mine hand unto the Lord, the most high God, the possessor of heaven and earth, That I will not take from a thread even to a shoelatchet, and that I will not take any thing that is thine, lest thou shouldest say, I have made Abram rich. -Genesis 14: 22-23

In these verses, this Patriarch was saying that he had already lifted up his hand to God in covenant. His connection was with his source, and his focus was on his source. By choosing to tithe all his spoil to Melchizedek and then telling the King of Sodom to take everything left after the tithe and the men's expenses, Abraham proved that he was not greedy or covetous. We will have to pass the same test. As God pours out ideas to make us prosper, we will have to prove we have integrity and that we are Kingdom-minded not money-minded. Let's keep our eyes on the source.

It's Never Too Late

One last lesson from Abraham the tither is that it is never too late to start over in the financial realm of your life. Even when you are fearful, even when you do things you ought not to, if you're in covenant with God, He will help you overcome your mistakes. You have not lived that long. You can have a new start. You have from here to eternity to enjoy the rewards of working according to His prosperous plan as He uses you to bless this world.

Stay Flexible to Secure Maximum Harvest

As we saw with Abraham, God had a plan to deliver Israel. How could 70 people living in Canaan amongst a multitude of Hittites physically possess the land? His plan, as He clearly told Abraham in Genesis 15, would take the seed of Abraham to Egypt to multiply in number.

> *And he said to Abram, Know of a surety that thy seed shall be a stranger in a land that is not theirs, and shall serve them; and they shall afflict them four hundred years; And also that nation, whom they shall serve, will I judge: and afterward shall they come out with great substance.... But in the fourth generation they shall come hither again: for the iniquity of the Amorites is not yet full. -Genesis 15:13-14, 16*

Configured in that plan was the life of one of Abraham's great-grandsons, Joseph. You can read the story of Joseph's life in Genesis 37-50. His life underwent varied and dramatic changes as he went from favored son to kidnap victim to slave to prisoner and, finally, to Prime Minister of Egypt. God orchestrated Joseph's life, and Joseph adapted to secure the maximum harvest for the seed of Abraham.

Like Joseph, you may need to be extricated from one position and put into another for maximum harvest to be secured. Be adaptable. God may need to pluck you out before He judges the company or industry in which you work. Get your résumé out, and do your part. The Holy Ghost can show you the things to come about your career, and He can take you safely out before He deals with your place of employment.

Divine Secrets to Preserve Your Crop

Behold, there come seven years of great plenty throughout all the land of Egypt: And there shall arise after them seven years of great famine; and all the plenty shall be forgotten in the land of Egypt.... And let them gather all the food of those good years that come, and lay up corn under the hand of Pharaoh, and let them keep food in the cities.
-Genesis 41:29-30, 35

Joseph had an idea from God on how to overcome during the time of famine destined for the nation of Egypt. God knows what the economy will do. He has given us the right as tithers to know things ahead of time and to be able to adjust. The Church should have known about 9/11 and not have suffered and been so unprepared. That great tragedy not only took the lives of thousands of Americans, but also affected the financial health of many more. Many churches, including my own, saw members suffer the loss of jobs, investments, or retirement income. That should not be. The Lord told Dr. Roberts, *"I'll protect your assets."* The protection of our assets is one of the benefits of tithing:

> *What are your assets? Anything of value to you, He'll protect.* ⌘

> *And I will rebuke the devourer for your sakes, and he shall not destroy the fruits of your ground; neither shall your vine cast her fruit before the time in the field, saith the Lord of hosts. -Malachi 3:11*

What are your assets? Your children, your spouse, your car, your investments, your lands—anything that is of value to you—He'll protect. That doesn't mean the devil won't try to steal, kill and destroy. It means you have a promise from God because you tithe and have seed in the ground. He may give you an idea and tell you where to move your assets for their protection, but He'll protect them and keep the eater from destroying them. Let us believe Him.

God's Idea Will Connect You with Strategic People

Genesis tells us that while Joseph was serving as Pharaoh's right-hand man, his father and brothers thought he was dead or enslaved. They were suffering through a famine in the Promised Land. Joseph's father, Jacob (Israel), thought: *"Maybe we ought to go to Egypt and buy corn."* It was a poured-out idea from God to intersect the paths of this family once again. Everything starts with an idea, and getting them out of the Promised Land and into Egypt was God's idea. He wanted to provide a place where they could multiply greatly before returning to the land He had promised Abraham. The coming famine on the earth was no threat to God's original plan.

We, too, are independent of the ups and downs of this world's economy, but do we act like it? Joseph's idea for a storehouse of grain to prepare for the seven years of famine and Israel's idea of sending his sons to Egypt to buy corn caused the paths of these two men to intersect. It also positioned the Jewish people for growth. God's ideas can position you in this coming time of harvest.

I believe the harvest is going to be in terms of months more than years. It will be a compressed and intense time of Kingdom activity. Just think what it would mean if you could come into that supernaturally compressed time of harvest with all your credit card debt out of the way. You would be free to move and free to help people, which is what the Church should do. We're to take up the slack and help people, but we don't have the cash. When the money does start rolling in, I believe we can be like Joseph and help set people in proper order financially. We can bring them out from under the oppressive weight of debt or help send them to go do what God has called them to do.

First the Book, Then the Idea

> *This book of the law shall not depart out of thy mouth; but thou shalt meditate therein day and night, that thou mayest observe to do according to all that is written therein: for then thou shall make thy way prosperous, and then thou shall have good success. -Joshua 1:8*

Essentially what God is telling Joshua is: Read your Bible. When you read the written Word of God, referred to in New Testament Greek as the *logos*, you receive information on the general will of God. Knowing God's general will is a prerequisite for hearing more specifically from God. It is only as you fill your heart and mind with the logos that God causes his Word to become the Greek word *rhema*, or living word, to you. At this point, you become aware that God is talking directly to you about a specific situation. So God was saying, first be a person of the logos before you can expect Me to give you an idea, or rhema, with more specific instructions. As Joshua meditated on the logos, God gave him the rhema needed to bring the children of Israel into the Promised Land. In fact, *any* idea that God gives you becomes a rhema word to you, whether it is scripture or not.

Just as He instructed Joshua, God is saying to us: Be a person of My Book, then I will deal with you after the Spirit. I will give you the way. I will give you the *ideas, concepts and insights* wherein you can make your way prosperous and have good success.

Get a Second Opinion

Of course, Moses worked on that same mission before Joshua. His early plans in its accomplishment included sending 12 men to spy out the land. Joshua himself had been one of the original spies sent out by Moses in Numbers 13, but only he and Caleb returned with a good report. The other 10 spies demoralized the Hebrew people with their bad report, and all the hope of the people evaporated. They saw themselves as grasshoppers and the sons of Anak as giants in the land: *"We be not able to go up against the people!"* (Numbers 13:32-33). But Joshua remembered the discouraging incident, and God gave him a better idea. He picked just two spies and sent them into Jericho where they finally lodged at the home of Rahab the harlot. This woman told them:

> *For we have heard how the Lord dried up the water of the Red sea for you, and what ye did unto the two kings of the Amorites... And as soon we had heard these things, our hearts did melt, neither did there remain any more courage in any man.... -Joshua 2:10-11*

Until these words of Rahab were reported to him by the spies returning from behind enemy lines, Joshua had no way of knowing what effect the very fear of them was having on the Canaanites. God was behind the discovery of that information. If the spies had not gone into Jericho, they would have lacked that strategic piece of wartime information. These spies told their leader upon their return, *"Let us go in at once for they are afraid of us."* Instead of having a bad report, Joshua received a good report because he acted on God's idea.

Even God's Natural Ideas Are Supernatural

As you can see, some ideas God pours out for tithers are natural, and some are supernatural. In other words, some are based in good logic, and others seem to make no sense. There was nothing supernatural about sending spies out on a reconnaissance mission; that was a natural idea. Other ideas that Joshua needed which God gave him, such as how to cross the Jordan at flood stage, were completely supernatural:

> **It shall come to pass, as soon as the soles of the feet of the priests that bear the ark of the Lord, the Lord of all the earth, shall rest in the waters of Jordan, that the waters of Jordan shall be cut off from the waters that come down from above; and they shall stand up on an heap.**
> **-Joshua 3:13**

Whether the idea He gives you is supernatural or natural, the power will be the same because He is the power source for every good and perfect idea from above. Whenever God says something and gives an idea, it is always supernatural in nature, even if it's natural. If He tells you to do something—whatever that something might be—and you do it, power is always applied. Your obedience to take Him at His Word has the same impact as Joshua hearing and obeying God's instructions to part the Jordan River! The same power is applied when *you* obey as it was when *Joshua* obeyed and led his people through the vast waters on dry ground. When you don't obey God, there is no power.

The next supernatural idea Joshua received from God was the plan to capture Jericho. This poured-out idea didn't look like such a brilliant military plan: walk around the city once a day for seven days without making a sound, and on the seventh day shout, and the walls will fall down!

Though it may not appear brilliant, God's military strategy for Jericho was brilliantly successful. If Joshua and his men had not waited for it, they would have failed. We need to note that even though Jesus in all his pre-millennial glory was present in the camp with them, they still needed God's idea and plan to take Jericho.

And it came to pass, when Joshua was by Jericho, that he lifted up his eyes and looked, and, behold, there stood a man over against him with his sword drawn in his hand: and Joshua went unto him, and said unto him, Art thou for us, or for our adversaries? And he said, Nay; but as captain of the host of the Lord am I now come…. -Joshua 5:13-14

As believers we have the presence of God, but His presence alone is not enough without an idea. Though we have the presence of God in a general way in our lives, it doesn't mean every human idea or plan we have will succeed. I have proved this out over and over in my own life. I would have a wonderful plan and saw no reason in the world why it should not succeed. God had to show me that if He didn't author it, it would fail. Sadly for me, I didn't pick up on this fact for so many years. I kept having my own ideas, but they didn't work. Only His ideas work.

Doing All: Whole Word and Whole Tithe

On the heels of their great victory at Jericho, the children of Israel had another opportunity to do the whole word and receive all the promises of success. They failed. They were beaten in their next military campaign at the little town of Ai, and when they asked the Lord why, He said:

> *Israel hath sinned, and they have also transgressed my covenant which I commanded them: for they have even taken of the accursed thing, and have also stolen, and dissembled also, and they have put it even among their own stuff. -Joshua 7:11*

Disobedience to God's Word—not *observing to do according to all that is written therein*—will cost us our prosperity and success. The instructions from the Lord to

Chapter Two: Old Testament Ingenuity

Israel were to burn everything in Jericho and touch none of the spoil. The silver, gold, brass and iron were to be brought into the Lord's treasury as a type of first-fruits offering to God, but a man named Achan sinned by taking some of the accursed things. His disobedience brought a stinging defeat to the entire people.

Apart from deliberate sin, can we miss it and continue? Yes, you are going to make a few mistakes as you begin to put *ideas, concepts and insights* into practice and work on ideas God has given you. You are going to miss it every now and then, but keep at it. Don't give up! You have a biblical right to God's ideas, and He wants to give you specific strategies to succeed.

I want to remind you that the Promised Land was filled with houses Israel did not build and fields they did not plant. They simply went in and occupied. They stepped right into position. God is doing that right now. He is getting the Church in position to possess His promises. Remember what God said to Dr. Roberts, *"My Church is out of position for the end-time harvest."* The Lord's desire is strong both for His harvest and for yours.

61

John Greiner

Chapter Three

This Way, Not That

The easiest way for me to show you how to get *ideas, concepts and insights* is to show you how I got it wrong. I tell my church: If I could, I would pay the price for you to get it right, but I can't. All I can do is tell you how I paid the price and what it took for me. There were times I fell on my face and I looked like a fool. Maybe you can see yourself in some of my failings, and you can learn from my mistakes. Learn, be blessed, and don't try this at home!

My Shepherd Calls Me by Name and Leads Me Out

In 1983, as a custom homebuilder, I heard my pastor say one Sunday, "How would you like to have banks come borrow money from you instead of you borrowing money from banks?" I had learned to listen to every word he said from the platform because I knew God spoke through him. Even if he said something that was outlandish, I'd listen to him. Though I knew my pastor was just a man otherwise, when he was on the platform, I recognized the mantle on his life and received from his anointing.

The words, "How would you like to have banks come borrow money from you instead of you borrowing money from banks?" spoke directly to me. In my profession, I made money off borrowed money. I would borrow money from the bank to build a house. Then when I'd sell it, hopefully, I would make enough to pay the bank back with interest and still have a little profit to put in my pocket. It all worked fine if the house sold right away. But if the house didn't sell right away, it didn't work very well at all. My pastor said those words, and I received them. I raised my hands there in church and said, "Lord, I thank you that *banks* are calling *me*."

With God as my witness, less than two weeks later a bank called me and said:

> *"Hey, John, we've got a problem here. The original builder has skipped town and left a custom home unfinished. The owners are very disgruntled and are threatening to end the contract."*
> *"What stage is the house in?" I asked.*
> *"Painted out with just a little left to finish."*
> *"Oh, yeah? The hardest part is what's left."*
> *"The hardest part? What do you mean?"*
> *"Well," I explained, "the difference between a monkey and a homebuilder is the last 20 percent. You know what I'm saying—getting all the little things in there and pleasing the customer."*
> *"We'll pay your expenses."*
> *"You'll pay me a fee on top of my expenses."*

I charged them $8000 for six weeks' work. That was not bad for them or for me. I finished that house, the clients moved in happy, and the bank was glad. The clients had a nice home. The bankers started talking, and I got another call from a different banker.

> *"Hey, John, I was talking to Mr. So-and-So at Allied Spelunker Bank. He said that you finished a house for them. We have two houses. The builder is broke and not doing anything. Will you come and finish them up?"*
> *"What stage are they in?"*
> *"Well, they are painted out."*
> *"It will cost you," I said smiling.*

It was the easiest work I have ever done. What was God doing? He was giving me an *idea* for a new business. All I had to do was to take that *idea* and make it *concept*. But I didn't do that.

If I had known then what I know now, I would have prayed and said, "Lord, I see this door is opening now. Show me how to implement it and develop it into a concept. Do you want me to develop a marketing plan to sell my services? I can go visit the banks that I know have an inventory of homes and offer a solution to their problems. How do I bring this into a *concept*, execute it and receive *insight*?"

That is how I should have done it. Those are the kinds of questions I should have put to the Lord to discover His plan for the open door. You can't just sit there and expect the phone to ring. God was merciful to ring my phone three times. He expects us to do something besides just wait for

Him to open the windows of heaven while we nap! I didn't do what I should have done. Instead, I plowed along doing just what I had always done: buying more lots and starting $1.4 million in new construction. The next thing I knew, the depression of 1984-85 hit the city of Houston. I went down the tubes.

Does Not Wisdom Call?

I remember the day I signed the contract to buy all the lots for those doomed homes. I remember having to override the Holy Ghost. I had an uneasy knot in the pit of my stomach during the whole business meeting, and when I picked up the pen to sign on the dotted line, it was as if I heard, "Don't do it!" ring out inside of me. You may wonder if business is spiritual. Well, it certainly is very practical. God is practical. Sometimes we try to spiritualize things to such a high degree that we think God doesn't get down to the nitty-gritty of life. He does, and giving us ideas to overcome in life is one of the ways He does it. If you don't act on the ideas, you are not being a good steward. You are despising what He is giving you to do. The idea is like a seed of small beginnings that you should not despise.

My problem was that I was too proud to do that kind of work. I wanted to be a builder of custom homes. I was convinced that because I was a tither, God was going to bless me just the way I'd planned. He was going to sell all those houses that I had decided to build. How wrong I was.

God saw the economic depression coming to my industry and geographic area. He was giving me another business with a nice cash flow, no debts, and no houses to sell. I would have been in a perfect position to go through a terrible economic time in the city of Houston and still come out on top.

Every builder friend of mine went broke, including me. The only people that survived were big homebuilding companies; the little guys didn't. I found out later that in one suburban neighborhood in West Houston alone, there were a staggering 1100 vacant lots for more than 18 months. One savings and loan had more than 300 properties sitting on the market.

If I had marketed myself to those bankers and said, "You know what? I can make sure the glass breakage is taken care of when kids vandalize your vacant properties. When the freezing weather comes, I can make sure the pipes are drained. I can keep the houses clean and lawns mown. When you've got a buyer, I can walk them through the house, make sure it closes, and fix all the little details to suit the customer." But no, I didn't do it.

God knew where my industry was headed, and He had a better path all arranged for me. I could have come out of my city's economic depression a rich man. I could have picked up some of those properties for pennies on the dollar and even owned my own real estate and mortgage companies.

If only I had followed that one idea that God dropped in my lap! I did it somewhat, but not to the full extent. Instead of trusting God, I got into presumption, following my own idea and overriding the Holy Ghost. For a season, my mistake put me out of position for financial wealth, but the experience did serve me a wealth of knowledge in the school of hard knocks. *Your* ideas will put you out of position, but *His* ideas will put you in position.

Favor Is a One-Way Street

One other lesson I learned is that favor is a one-way street. It only flows in the direction of God's will for you. It is a specific benefit that comes from a specific direction. He does not give you *carte blanche* favor with everybody and everything in all cases. He gives you specific, precision favor in the direction He wants to bless. If you go in your direction, you're going to have a hard time. If you go in His direction, it is already blessed.

Several years later, I was out driving and praying, and I drove by a house under construction in a Houston suburb. It was framing up. I got out of my car, smelled that lumber, and I had a great desire to build houses again. I had been so disappointed when I lost my home-building business, and I was sure I would never build houses again. Yet after almost four years, God put the desire back in my heart.

I looked out at all the vacant lots around me—hundreds and hundreds of vacant lots. I began to pray, "Well, Lord, that is one thing that I could do. I could go over and put houses on them. I could help the mortgage company." I was still trying to find the plan of God for my business.

Opening the Two-Leaved Gates

One Sunday I was talking with a friend of mine after church, and he mentioned West University Place, an upscale urban neighborhood bordering the Texas Medical Center and Rice University. When he said it, boom! I got a witness, and I couldn't shake it. The next day, there was an article about this neighborhood in the newspaper. It seemed like there was sign after sign of God's favor pointing me in that direction. Still, I would need start-up capital to begin building again. In my morning prayer time, this scripture came alive in my spirit:

> ***Thus saith the Lord to his anointed, to Cyrus, whose right hand I have holden, to subdue nations before him; and I will loose the loins of kings, to open before him the two leaved gates; and the gates shall not be shut; I will go before thee, and make the crooked places straight: I will break in pieces the gates of brass, and cut in sunder the bars of iron: And I will give thee the treasures of darkness, and hidden riches of secret places, that thou mayest know that I, the Lord, which call thee by thy name, am the God of Israel. -Isaiah 45:1-3***

I knew God would supply the money I needed. Of course, I thought it would come directly into my checking account! Instead, God brought me a financial partner. During our initial meeting, I drove to his home, and the street name had the word "king" in it. I just smiled. When I pulled into his driveway, he had an ornate double-gate which literally opened before me. Though I had been to his home before, God used those details at that moment to confirm His plan for me.

One day, my partner and I decided to begin driving through "West U" to scout it out. Building in that neighborhood was an *idea* from God that I had to study into in order to develop into a *concept*. I investigated the housing market in that neighborhood and found that every house was red brick and looked like a cube. They all looked the same, and at the price they were selling, I couldn't see how we could make any profit. I began to pray for God to give me the steps to go from *idea* to successful *concept.*

Hidden Riches in Secret Places

What exactly was I going to build? The reason the houses in that area were all little cubes of red brick was because they were built on lots only 50 feet wide. Once you put a driveway in, the width available for the house decreased even further resulting in homes with tiny bedrooms, tiny closets and tiny bathrooms—even in the master suite. The tiny dimensions looked like a doll's house compared to the spacious homes I had built in Houston's suburbs. Would we make a profit off of these red-brick cubes?

I consulted with a plan designer and told him my situation. He came up with a concept: a *porte-cochère.* Create a covered driveway, he said, and build out part of the home's upstairs area over the driveway. This would allow for bigger bedrooms and closets. The only drawback was that this design required an oversized lot. We went ahead and had some plans drawn. Soon God provided an oversized lot that only had an old house perfect for demolition, and we built our prototype house. Not only did it sell before it was finished saving money on interest costs, but we set a neighborhood record for the highest price-per-square foot. That was a poured-out blessing from a poured-out idea, and it was marvelous in my sight. Using the same method, my partner and I built the second house of that type, sold it before completion, and set new real estate records all over again.

This one idea from heaven turned a profit, and my company made money from it for several years. But, frankly, I did not see the connection with tithing, nor did I realize an idea sometimes only works for a season. We need fresh ideas as seasons change and old ideas fail to work as before. We live in a changing world, and we must depend on the Lord.

Notice what I did in this one instance of getting it right: I observed God's rhema to me to do *all that was written therein*, and His Spirit led me step by step. I stayed on favor's one-way street as I took a poured-out idea, brought it into a concept, developed it into a lifestyle that made my way prosperous, having very good success.

John Greiner

Chapter Four

Spirit-Led Spending

In our study of ideas, concepts and insights we have focused on the income side of God's poured-out ideas for every tither. The Bible examples we have examined—Abraham, Isaac, Jacob, Joseph and Joshua—have all addressed the issue of money coming into your hands and how your income can be increased. But what about the expense side, the issue of money leaving your hands? God wants to give you revelation about this side of your finances as well. In many instances, your spending must be set in order and good stewardship proven before He will release increase on the income side. The importance of your outgo in the plans and purposes of God is revealed in His words to Dr. Roberts:

> *Not only has the income been hindered, but the outgo is too much debt. Debt has strangled the Church, putting my people out of position and bringing them into bondage. The credit system of this world has bound them and brought them into crisis debt. -Dr. Oral Roberts*

If your outgo is not under the leadership of the Holy Ghost and you're not walking according to the Spirit in your spending, you will be out of position for what God wants to do in these last days. Wake up! Part of getting in position is putting God first and putting what He wants ahead of what our flesh wants. We are spending money on things not sanctioned by His Spirit and going into debt just to bless *ourselves*. When we bless *ourselves* and insist that, "I deserve this," the blessing of the *Lord* (which would have come had we waited) goes up in a puff of smoke.

Regardless of whether you pay with cash or credit, you need to guard against using money to gratify fleshly desires. This means that before you pull out your wallet on a major purchase, check to make sure your heart is right and your money is yielded to God first. Just for the moment, put away the sensual appeal or seeming necessity of the item, and give God a chance to give you a thumbs-up or thumbs-down. It's good to wait until you're absolutely sure you have peace in your spirit before sealing the deal. God is much smarter than you. He sees ahead of you, and He always has your best interests at heart. Just by an inner witness, many times you can know whether you should spend, save, invest, or wait.

There are Christians at every income level who max out their lifestyle, living paycheck to paycheck. Everything may go along fine for awhile, but as soon as life throws the slightest curve, they're sucked into the undercurrent of lack and swept out into a sea of insufficiency. The truth is that we don't *deserve* anything. You only receive what you have *sown* to. When you have *sown* to it, God is going to let you know, "It's due season. You've got a harvest coming in." The Lord will give you the right pathway to reap your ripe harvest and avoid crop failure. Proverbs 10:22 says, ***"The***

blessing of the Lord, it maketh rich, and he addeth no sorrow with it.*"*

Reaping Right on Time

Your tithes and offerings are your financial seed, and the size of your harvest corresponds to the amount of the seed you sow. Luke 6:38 says it this way: *"... with the same measure that ye mete withal it shall be measured to you again."*

Reaping your financial harvest means that you bring it into the tangible world either for consumption or to sow for your next crop. You're picking the fruit from your spiritual tree. Reaping can entail anything from asking your boss for a raise to plunking down money for a new home. Timing is key, and we need ideas from God about when and how to proceed in life's affairs. God is well able to communicate with you in ways that you can understand:

> **But he that entereth in by the door is the shepherd of the sheep. To him the porter openeth; and the sheep hear his voice: and he calleth his own sheep by name, and leadeth them out. And when he putteth forth his own sheep, he goeth before them, and the sheep follow him: for they know his voice. -John 10:2-4**

Pray and believe God that you will recognize His voice regarding financial matters. If you'll follow His leading, He will show you *when* to reap, *where* to reap, and give you step-by-step guidance on *how* to bring in your harvest.

> *...So is the kingdom of God, as if a man should cast seed into the ground; And should sleep, and rise night and day, and the seed should spring and grow up, he knoweth not how. For the earth bringeth forth fruit of herself; first the blade, then the ear, after that the full corn in the ear. But when the fruit is brought forth, immediately he putteth in the sickle, because the harvest is come. -Mark 4:26-29*

Kingdom blessings operate on the seed-sowing principle, but notice the required process of patience and preparation before your full harvest comes. You sow a seed; sleep and rise, night and day; then, suddenly, a crop begins to come up, first the blade, then the ear. Can you do anything with the blade? No! How much can you buy at the mall with just a blade? Can you do anything with the ear? Very little. Only when the corn is ripe, do you immediately put in the sickle to reap. If it is not ripe when you put in the sickle, you won't have much, and what little you do have won't be good. You can't plant it, and you certainly don't want to eat it.

I planted corn one time. I tried to wait the right amount of time, but one day, when I just couldn't stand it any longer, I picked an ear and shucked it. It was a green, slimy mess inside. I managed to wait another whole week before I went and picked another ear. Inside were hard, tiny kernels. At the end of all my waiting, I got one ear out of the entire stalk of corn, and that one ear was barely 6 inches long. That tiny insufficient ear reminds me of the lack and shortfall in our lives when we try to have financial success on our own schedule.

You need the Holy Ghost to tell you when your crop is ready. He can help you to be spirit-dominant and not flesh-dominant when it comes to buying so you won't get into the position of blessing *yourself.* Blessing yourself is the pathway of presumption, and it takes you from *I-want-this* to *I-deserve-that.* Eventually you're willing to go into debt to get that thing, no matter the consequence. The presumption pathway will always have you heading in the wrong direction, running ahead of the Lord's blessing, and failing to apply the principles of the Kingdom in your life. Kingdom principles, on the other hand, always bring

> *Patience and self-control will help you maximize your harvest.*
>
> ⌘

blessings and lead you into paths of abundance and fullness. I've learned this the hard way, and following God's lead about purchasing is so important for every believer.

I remember when I saw a custom van and simply *had* to have it. My nose longed for the "new car smell" of the plush interior. I had the money, and I paid cash for it. I didn't actually bother to check with the Lord about that purchase. I just assumed that my having the cash was a sign this deal was from God. I didn't have to borrow the money. I simply wrote out a check. I bought that van brand new with all the bells and whistles on it, and I never will forget how I felt driving it every day. It was noisy and uncomfortable. After all, it was a van, so I was sitting right over the front wheel, feeling every bump in the road. I didn't like it. It wasn't long before I began to regret buying it. God knows what we need more than we do ourselves. If I had only waited, I'm convinced God would have put me into something better suited for me. Make no mistake, my own flesh had deceived me into buying that van.

> *Be not deceived; God is not mocked: for whatsoever a man soweth, that shall he also reap. For he that soweth to his flesh shall of the flesh reap corruption; but he that soweth to the Spirit shall of the Spirit reap life everlasting.*
> *-Galatians 6:7-8*

Be not deceived. That is what the Lord told the disciples over and over when they asked, "When are you coming back, Lord?" He would say: "Take heed that you be not deceived." Deception in these last days has gotten the Church out of position and into massive debt. I am not referring to simple car or home loans. I am referring to credit card debt and other types of debt that have us so choked, so stressed and pressured that we have no hope nor do we know what to do.

Of course, I realize that you may not pay off your mortgage and clear out all your debt by tomorrow through this teaching, but my heart is to see everyone set free from the weight of *unnecessary* debt. The truth I received in Dr. Roberts' living room has the power to deliver God's people from bondage, and as a steward of that truth, I want you to wake up to the good news about your financial future. Do not allow mistakes on the outgo side, like early reaping, to hinder your harvest.

Fighting Crop Failure

Even if you are tithing and believing God for His poured-out *ideas, concepts and insights,* you will still have to fight crop failure. All too often, harvest is compromised when we allow ourselves to get tricked into using credit for the wrong reasons. The credit system in this country strives to suck you in and get all your money, as the Lord's words to Dr. Roberts forcefully stated. Let's look at ways to escape from the system's trickery and discover how to stop ensnaring ourselves. Changing the way we think is the first step to changing our situation and reaping our full harvest.

A compromised harvest is a type of costly crop failure that the Bible warns us about. In Mark 4, there are three conditions guaranteed to produce crop failures in our fields:

> *...Behold, there went out a sower to sow: And it came to pass, as he sowed, some fell by the way side, and the fowls of the air came and devoured it up.*
>
> *And some fell on stony ground, where it had not much earth: and immediately it sprang up, because it had no depth of earth: But when the sun was up, it was scorched; and because it had no root, it withered away.*
>
> *And some fell among thorns, and the thorns grew up, and choked it, and it yielded no fruit.*
> *-Mark 4:3-7*

Notice that this last type of sowing—sowing among thorns—was fruitful initially. Everything was going along fine for a while. Fruitful became unfruitful when three things entered the heart of the person cultivating the seed:

> *And these are they which are sown among thorns; such as hear the word,*
>
> *And the cares of this world, and the deceitfulness of riches, and the lusts of other things entering in, choke the word, and it becometh unfruitful. -Mark 4:18-19*

The lust or desire for other things may start as an innocent pastime and develop into a care or concern that has nothing to do with the Kingdom of God. Though there is nothing wrong with golf, there are preachers who have become more concerned with their golf game than with what they are going to preach. You can see how this type of mentality could crop up with any pastime, as people are willing to spend increasingly more time and money chasing their own leisure. Distractions that were once tolerable twenty years ago aren't always in our best interests today. We need to keep a Kingdom focus in these end-times.

Throughout my Christian life, I have taken periodic breaks alone in order to seek the Lord in prayer. During one of these times recently, the Holy Ghost spoke to me and said that many are *satiated* (that is the word He used) with the pleasures of this world and with the cares of this world. And most of this world's cares come from the pursuit of the pleasures. *Satiated* means "being gorged to repletion, resulting in destruction of interest or desire." We can be so gorged, so filled up with other things, that we lose interest in the Kingdom of God, and it becomes a lower, lesser priority.

Pursuing the pleasures of the world means our desire is for things other than the Kingdom. Our attempt to pay for all our pursuits brings the cares of the world down on us. So you see the sad but certain connection between choking the Word of God and the unfruitfulness of debt. Though it hurts, you have to be open before God about the parts of your life where flesh has intervened and taken the lead instead of the Spirit. If you go ahead and plead guilty, mercy can come and bring with it a fresh start.

Lust of the Flesh

This type of crop failure explains how you can tithe without receiving the associated blessings. Though you have a biblical right to receive God's ideas as a tither, if your focus is solely on pursuing pleasure, you may not receive those ideas. The thorns of the cares of the world can keep you from hearing God's idea and God's plan. Because the thorns, or lusts of other things, act as a sort of barrier, they choke off the ideas and keep them from coming to fruition in your life. You can't have it both ways, as Jesus said:

> *No man can serve two masters: for either he will hate the one, and love the other; or else he will hold to the one, and despise the other. Ye cannot serve God and mammon. -Matthew 6:24*

I can look back at my life and trace a direct correlation between walking in the flesh and financial mistakes:

So then they that are in the flesh cannot please God. But ye are not in the flesh, but in the Spirit, if so be that the Spirit of God dwell in you…. Therefore, brethren, we are debtors, not to the flesh, to live after the flesh. For if ye live after the flesh, ye shall die: but if ye through the Spirit do mortify the deeds of the body, ye shall live. For as many as are led by the Spirit of God, they are the sons of God.
-Romans 8:8-9, 12-14

It says, *"Therefore, brothers, we are debtors"*–so we should be debtors, but not to the flesh to live after the flesh's desire or leading. We are debtors to live to the Spirit. We owe it all to God to walk according to the Spirit. To the degree that we pay our debt to Him and live according to His Spirit, we will enjoy a life free from any thorns choking off our supply.

Lust of the Eyes

The credit system is designed to appeal to the lust of the eyes, the lust of the flesh, and the pride of life. When we allow ourselves to go down that path, we will fall into snares. Have we been hard enough on ourselves?

Love not the world, neither the things that are in the world. If any man love the world, the love of the Father is not in him. For all that is in the world, the lust of the flesh, and the lust of

the eyes, and the pride of life, is not of the
Father, but is of the world. And the world
passeth away, and the lust thereof: but he that
doeth the will of God abideth for ever.
-1 John 2:15-17

The world's credit system, as the Lord referred to it through Dr. Roberts, is primarily designed to ensnare you with the things of this world and to get you in competition with others, whether it's your neighbors (the proverbial Joneses) or fellow believers. The only *ideas, concepts and insights* you'll get with that kind of heart motivation will be born out of covetousness over what others have. The Lord is not going to fund the ideas you come up with that have nothing to do with His love and are born off the lust of the flesh, the lust of the eyes and the pride of life.

Tithing to the Wind

And these are they by the way side, where the
word is sown; but when they have heard, Satan
cometh immediately, and taketh away the word
that was sown in their hearts. -Mark 4:15

Like the seed falling by the wayside, many people throw their money out to the four winds. They don't even think about where they are sending their tithe. Some tithe to dead churches and watch Christian TV to fill in blanks in their spiritual diet. They may occasionally visit a live church and say, "Well, you know my church is dead, but God has not released me. I'll keep tithing to my dead church and pray that things will change over there." It is not scriptural for you to stay there and pray against what your pastor is doing. If that is your pastor, you must either agree with him and support him, or you must get out of there. If you do want to pray for change in your church, you must pray in the Holy Ghost for your pastor and not merely according to your will for him to change. If things are so bad at your home church that you feel like attending another church to get fed, your tithe to your dead home church is not going to produce a crop. You are throwing your seed by the wayside.

Stony Ground

> *And these are they likewise which are sown on stony ground; who, when they have heard the word, immediately receive it with gladness; And have no root in themselves, and so endure but for a time: afterward, when affliction or persecution ariseth for the word's sake, immediately they are offended. -Mark 4:16-17*

This type of crop failure describes people with no endurance, who, under heat of circumstances, quickly give up. With no spiritual grit, they are totally circumstance-led. Oh, they sow that seed with many initial Hallelujahs and rejoicing; "Yes, amen, I walk by faith and not by sight!" But, the first time the devil brings opposition, their shout can change into, "I can't tithe any more; I can't afford to tithe."

Mega Crop Failure: No Tithe

Nothing can hinder a harvest like not tithing! Obedience to the Word of God is a prerequisite for blessing. God told the Israelites that He required their obedience and whole-hearted service to Him in order to send rain upon their crops:

> *And it shall come to pass, if ye shall hearken diligently unto my commandments which I command you this day, to love the Lord your God, and to serve him with all your heart and with all your soul, That I will give you the rain of your land in his due season, the first rain and the latter rain, that thou mayest gather in thy corn, and thy wine, and thine oil. And I will send grass in thy fields for thy cattle, that thou mayest eat and be full. -Deuteronomy 11:13-15*

As with the Israelites, serving God with all your heart includes serving Him with your money, and your obedience to Him brings your rain and your harvest. I am not suggesting that you can't make it at all if you don't tithe. There are certain things that work in the natural realm. If you go to work, then you'll get paid, and you won't starve to death just because you don't tithe. Here, we see the deceitfulness of certain ways of thinking in the Body of Christ. Since people do manage to get by without tithing, there remains a large contingent of believers who think they don't need to tithe. Don't be mistaken: the benefits of tithing go far beyond the financial realm.

"Bring ye all the tithe into the storehouse, that there may be meat in mine house," God says. The Old Testament priests lived off the tithes from the people of Israel, and a portion of it fed them. Correspondingly, if you don't tithe, there will not be meat in the house of God for your spirit to eat. You need spiritual nourishment, and it comes first from the storehouse of your local church where your local pastor preaches and feeds you. From a spiritual standpoint, your capacity to receive nourishment from your church is directly proportionate to your obedience in tithing. From a practical standpoint, if your pastor draws an income from your tithe and others, he doesn't have to sweat out a living from this world. Instead, he can serve the vital role of feeding his flock, devoting himself continually to prayer and to the ministry of the Word (Acts 6:4) for your benefit. What's more, Malachi 3 states that you rob God when you don't tithe, and money isn't the only thing you withhold from Him. He is robbed of the pleasure He has in blessing you. *"Fear not, little flock,"* Jesus says in Luke 12:32, *"for it is your Father's good pleasure to give you the kingdom."*

Then there are those Dr. Roberts mentioned who tithe incorrectly. You don't take the tithe, pray, and say, "What do I do with it this month?" The tithe belongs to your storehouse. Some want to give their tithes to unsaved relatives who are going through tough times. Another person may want to take the tithe and pay her daughter's tuition in Bible school. I had a friend who would take his tithe and go feed the poor. That is not tithing. If the recipients aren't providing you the covering of a local church, they don't qualify as a storehouse. Offerings over and above your tithe can go to any other ministry in any way the Holy Ghost directs you.

Is Debt Sin?

During our time together, Dr. Roberts repeatedly quoted the heart of God about debt and the Church. Debt is getting the Church off the right pathway to harvest and out of position for what God wants to do. Is all debt sin? I don't think so, nor do I think borrowing is a sin, but it must be sanctioned by the Holy Ghost. What is debt? The Jewish concept of debt was that you owed someone and you couldn't pay them. If you were able to meet your obligations to pay, you were not in debt, nor were you considered to be a debtor. Therefore, having a home or car loan does not make you a debtor so long as you are able to make the loan payments.

However, if you have to borrow money to make ends meet, your obligations exceed your ability to pay them. Let's say that you have a certain amount of credit card debt, a home loan, and insurance payments on the outgo side. On the other side, you have an income. If your outgo exceeds your income, you're in debt. If last year, you had a certain amount of debt, and this year there is more debt and not less, you may risk outstripping your ability to repay.

If you're in debt, you have to find a way to increase your income or reduce your outgo. Preferably you can do both of these things at the same time. It is simple and not hard. When it comes to the debt issue, the gospel to the poor is good news: we don't have to live in debt. We can make the necessary changes, and God will give us a financial miracle.

One essential change: stop all unnecessary purchasing. If you can possibly live without it, don't buy it. Find ways to save money every day, then use those savings to pay off your credit card balances. For example, don't take your family to a restaurant, pay with a credit card, and then make only a couple of dollars minimum payment each month. Experts say if you're already carrying a balance on your card and make only minimum payments, it could take 20 years to pay off, even if you never charge anything again. You could pay more in interest than the meal originally cost. Obviously that hamburger isn't worth it. Make sandwiches at home!

You must be wiser in your use of credit. If you are disciplined and have not gone into great debt, you can use a credit card to help you. If there is a medical emergency or your car breaks down, and you don't have enough cash to pay the whole thing before your next payday, it is not a sin to put that expense on a credit card. In fact, it is nice to have one. I have been where I didn't have a credit card, and it wasn't easy to operate in this world. Some people link credit cards with the Pharaoh system. Like Pharaoh beat the children of Israel, forcing them to make more and more bricks with less and less hay, powerful banks use ballooning interest and fees to force unwitting borrowers into hard labor. Still, I believe your good credit rating can be a blessing if you know how to win the game. Just make sure you act responsibly when you do use a credit card.

> *Qualify for a financial miracle by recognizing and admitting where you've been in the flesh.*
>
> ⌘

But what if you find yourself up to your ears in debt? Your cards are all charged up, and bills seem to stuff your mailbox? Everybody has a story, whether it was 9/11 or a job lay-off. As you've read, I went through a massive home-building depression in the mid-80s, and God tried to pluck me out of it with ideas that I didn't pursue. We've all missed ideas and found ourselves in the soup one way or another, but what can you do now? Can everyone who needs a financial miracle get one and be set free from the horrible weight of debt?

Qualify for a Financial Miracle

You can meet the requirements and obtain your financial miracle by walking in the Spirit, tithing, and believing for *ideas, concepts and insights.* Even though the devil may try to convince you that you cannot tithe because of debt, being a tither is the main qualification for your miracle; God gives tithers ideas about how to get out of debt. Remember, too, that God will require discipline. After all, a disciple is a *disciplined one.*

You might find it helpful to do what I did. Get all your credit cards statements; go through all the bills from three years back or whenever it all started; look at all the individual charges, and call them like they really are: "This was *flesh*; this was a *necessity. Flesh, flesh,"* etc. Quit avoiding the truth. I've found in my own disasters that God will honor your honesty if you look in the mirror and say, "The buck stops here." Qualify for a financial miracle by recognizing and admitting where you have been in the flesh.

Put everything out on the table, and show Him everything you've done. Be open. Don't hide behind anything. Instead of making excuses, own up to your mistakes, and let His mercy come on you. He will always give you mercy, but only if you confess. Find out your contribution to the mess and simply repent. *Repent* means to change your mind and your actions. To begin a renewed walk in the Spirit, you will have to cleave to the fruit of the Spirit of *temperance*, another word for self-control. Find ways to stop spending what you don't have and buying what you don't need. Correct your outgo.

Chapter Five

A New Start

Whether you have credit card debt from a few unwise purchases or you are facing financial devastation, let this point mark your new start as we find the place where financial miracles are written for us in the Bible. God helped people who were in debt over their heads and without hope. The Spirit of the Lord brings good news to every part of your life that is poor or lacking. The time of His favor is now. He wants you to live a life of peace and to be free from financial stress and care.

Let's look at God's Word to the prophet Elijah concerning provision for himself and a starving widow:

> *Get thee hence, and turn thee eastward, and hide thyself by the brook Cherith, that is before Jordan. And it shall be, that thou shalt drink of the brook; and I have commanded the ravens to feed thee there....*
>
> *And the ravens brought him bread and flesh in the morning, and bread and flesh in the evening; and he drank at the brook. And it*

*came to pass after a while, that the brook dried
up, because there had been no rain in the land.
And the word of the Lord came to him, saying,
Arise, get thee to Zarephath, which belongeth
to Zidon, and dwell there: behold, I have
commanded a widow woman there to sustain
thee.' -I Kings 17:3, 6-9*

The widow of Zarephath was poor and at her wits' end. She was not Jewish, so she had no legal covenant or standing with God.   Still, God knew her address, and He even sent His prophet to her house.

On the other side of the equation was Elijah who had pronounced judgment on the Northern Kingdom by prophesying drought on the land. Now he was forced to live in the midst of the very judgment God used him to pronounce. God gave His prophet these directions to a place of provision: Go to the brook Cherith, and a raven will bring Sloppy-Joes (bread and flesh) twice a day. This went on until the brook dried up.

Provision's New Address

For some of you, the brook has dried up. Some people are staying in churches or jobs where there's been no provision for a very long time. God told Elijah He had another place for him and that He had commanded a widow woman to feed him. Based on God's instructions, Elijah may have thought the woman would be rich and live in a mansion. Maybe she would have lots of servants to care for his every need. Instead Elijah arrives to find her picking up sticks to make her last meal and die. God's choice was a desperate woman in deep financial distress who couldn't do anything for Elijah in the natural:

> *So he arose and went to Zerephath. And when he came to the gate of the city, behold, the widow woman was there gathering of sticks: and he called to her, and said, Fetch me, I pray thee, a little water in a vessel, that I may drink. And as she was going to fetch it, he called to her, and said, Bring me, I pray thee, a morsel of bread in thine hand. And she said, As the Lord thy God liveth, I have not a cake, but an handful of meal in a barrel, and a little oil in a cruse: and, behold, I am gathering two sticks, that I may go in and dress it for me and my son, that we may eat it, and die. -I Kings 17:10-12*

Notice what the prophet said to her. In spite of her circumstances (poor enough to pick up sticks) and her words ("I am going to pick up sticks to bake my last meal and die."), Elijah asked, "Can you give me a little water?" He was probing to see if he could get her to do anything of faith. She agreed, and when she passed the test of his first probing, he brought out the bigger test: "Bring me a morsel of bread."

Elijah wasn't just interested in taking from the widow woman; he wanted to give her something—something far bigger than the morsel he first asked of her. Elijah gave her a promise from God:

> *...Fear not; go and do as thou has said: but make me thereof a little cake first, and bring it*

***unto me, and after make for thee and for thy
son. For thus saith the Lord God of Israel, The
barrel of meal shall not waste, neither shall the
cruse of oil fail, until the day that the Lord
sendeth rain up on the earth. -I Kings 17:13-14***

It Always Pays to Put God First

You, too, have a promise when you put God first. This Old Testament example of putting the prophet first is a type and shadow of our tithing and putting God first. When you're in heavy debt, the devil will tell you that you can't tithe. You may have to call your creditors and tell them you need more time to work things out, but don't stop tithing. If you're not tithing, go ahead and start tithing now. If your accountant tells you tithing will bring financial ruin in your predicament, find a different accountant who understands the importance of the tithe.

In the prior passage, God gave His promise to a widow woman who had no covenant: put Me first, I'll put you first. He will do the same for tithers today as He pours out *ideas, concepts and insights* to bring us out of debt and into provision for every need.

This non-Jewish woman who acted on God's promise also stands as an example of how unbelievers can tithe and get blessed in this world's goods. A number of them have discovered this principle, and they are actively putting it to practice and benefiting from it. There are unsaved men who are seeing the blessing that comes from their believing wives' tithing of the household money and are deciding to let them tithe on the entire family income: "Well, if it works for you, I'll let you tithe mine, too." They do well, but what does it profit a man if he gains the whole world and loses his own soul? Tithing is a spiritual law, and—like the natural law of gravity—it works for believers and non-believers alike.

> *And she went and did according to the saying*
> *of Elijah: and she, and he, and her house, did*
> *eat many days. And the barrel of meal wasted*
> *not, neither did the cruse of oil fail, according*
> *to the word of the Lord, which he spake by*
> *Elijah. -I Kings 17:15-16*

As soon as she obeyed the Word of the Lord and tithed a little cake first to the prophet, an 18-wheeler pulled up to her front door, right? It had 13 tons of meal and 150 barrels of oil, and the driver asked her where he could unload all her provision for the next year. No! Nothing visible happened. There was no immediate evidence of the provision that God had promised if she obeyed Him in the tithe. The widow lady just went down, scooped some meal, and poured out some oil, day after day after day after day. She did it every day for a year, and it never ran out.

Positioned for Supernatural Supply

The Bible doesn't state that she received a great abundance all of a sudden. It just tells us that the provision did not waste, go down, or dry up. Every time she made a demand on what little she had, it proved to be enough to meet the need. God multiplied and extended what she had, and His prophet got her in position to receive supernatural supply.

Today, God often uses apostles in His Body to put us in position. In fact, this is one major purposeof the apostolic anointing and mantle in the Church. It is evident through both of the *Wake-Up Call* visitations, for example, that Dr. Roberts, a general of the faith, is warning us that we're not ready for the second coming of Jesus. God's mercy is giving us a second chance to prepare ourselves, both spiritually and financially, to labor in His end-time harvest fields. Those of us who are entangled and ensnared financially should not feel forgotten by God. On the contrary, He still knows the address of those of us looking for sticks in Zarephath, and He wants each one of us in position so that he can use us to bring more souls into His Kingdom.

During the time of famine, the widow in I Kings and her entire household had enough to eat. In a time when price gouging could potentially drive up the cost of everything, she never had to buy her meal or oil at inflated black-market prices. A miracle put her in position to overcome fluctuations in the economy of her nation.

I believe there are times coming on the earth when it will become even more critical to walk according to the Spirit, and only those in position will have enough natural and spiritual food to eat. Being in position will also make us unshakeable no matter the attack, and—unlike 9/11—we won't be caught unaware.

Chapter Six

Protecting and Growing Your Assets

What's in the House?

Now there cried a certain woman of the wives of the sons of the prophets unto Elisha, saying, Thy servant my husband is dead; and thou knowest that thy servant did fear the Lord: and the creditor is come to take unto him my two sons to be bondmen. -II Kings 4:1

In this passage we find another person in deep, life-threatening debt. Also a widow, her husband had been one of the prophets, and she asked Elisha, "What I am going to do? The creditors are coming to take away my boys." For a widow to lose her boys meant she would lose her livelihood because sons could work and earn a living to support their mother. Financially, this was a life-and-death situation that meant the destruction of her family, with the children to be sold into slavery.

> *And Elisha said unto her, What shall I do for*
> *thee? Tell me, what hast thou in the house?*
> *–II Kings 4:2a*

The devil will tell you that you "ain't got nothing and you can't tithe." The truth is we all have something. This woman had to think for a moment and take inventory:

> *And she said, Thine handmaid hath not any*
> *thing in the house, save a pot of oil.*
> *-II Kings 4:2b*

That little pot of oil seemed to be nothing, considering that she owed $100,000 at an interest rate of 19.8 percent! There was no way for her to pay it, and they were coming to get her boys.

> *Then he said, Go, borrow thee vessels abroad of*
> *all thy neighbours, even empty vessels; borrow*
> *not a few. -II Kings 4:3*

In other words, Elisha was saying, "Don't skimp on the number of vessels. Borrow as many as you can. Get your boys, shut the door, and start pouring out." This widow had enough sense to do as Elisha the prophet said, though it must have sounded foolish to her. If she only had a little pot of oil, why would she need all those vessels?

The Foolish Things

In a desperate financial situation, sometimes the Lord will tell you to do things that don't make sense in the natural in order to give you a supernatural solution. I remember one time when I had suffered a business loss and I couldn't pay my bills, I had people standing in line to turn me down for a job. I'd go apply for employment, and they'd look at the application and tell me that I was *over-qualified*. I was so over-qualified I felt downright under-qualified. I guess I could have told my creditors that I was too over-qualified to get a job and pay them what I owed.

One day a friend of mine asked if I knew anyone who wanted to work for $6.50 an hour. Immediately in my heart, I knew he was talking about me! Me? Work for $6.50 an hour? What in the world could he be thinking? I told him that I didn't know anyone, but I'd call if someone came to mind. I had a mechanical engineering degree and had owned my own business for many years. Besides, I had a wife and two kids to support. Why would he think I'd work for $6.50 an hour?

The very next morning in prayer the Lord and I had a conversation:

> *"So, you're too proud to work for $6.50 an hour?"*
> *"No sir. No, I am not."*
> *"Well, you better call that guy before he hires somebody else."*

I was hired, and within a week I received a pay raise to the high-cotton sum of $8.50 an hour!

My job was to put racks in the convenience store refrigerator coolers to hold chocolate candy bars. The purpose of my job was so that people who came into the gas stations could see the nearly frozen candy bars hanging next to the soft drinks and buy them. I was convinced that dentists paid the stores money for the steady flow of patients needing their teeth fixed after eating those bricks of candy.

As you can imagine, the job didn't require a lot of smarts, but I sure felt good getting a paycheck. Though it looked like an insignificant amount, I was glad to finally have some money to tithe. After suffering my own personal famine for some time, it felt good to be able to pay *something* to *somebody*. If I had turned down that foolish-looking job "opportunity," who knows what would have happened. After a couple of months, I got an offer for a better-paying position, and I'm convinced this little job served as a stepping stone. Sometimes we want everything instantly, but when you're out of the will of God like I was in those years, it takes a little stepping to get back in it.

Though this job seemed futile to me at first compared to the vast debt and need in my life, God met me where I was in order to multiply my provision. As with Elisha's widow sent to gather pots, our obedience in the small things counts big with God. It can spark the flame of supernatural supply.

> *And it came to pass, when the vessels were full, that she said unto her son, Bring me yet a vessel. And he said unto her, There is not a vessel more. And the oil stayed. Then she came and told the man of God. And he said,*

Go, sell the oil, and pay thy debt, and live thou
and thy children of the rest. -II Kings 4:6-7

Now, here was abundance. "Pay your debts, and live off the rest," the prophet said. Not only did she have food for a year like the first widow, she had it for the rest of her life. This is a higher level of provision, and, not surprisingly, it was due to her status as a tither. This status was conferred on her because her late husband, one of the prophets, would certainly have tithed. In a sense, his tithing saw her through after his death, and in the same way, your tithing will bless your posterity and deliver them from impossible situations.

Protection and Multiplication

Another promise for tithers, as the Lord told Dr. Roberts, is the protection of your assets. In Malachi 3, didn't God say He will rebuke the devourer for your sake? God will safeguard you when you are caught in a financial whirlwind. For the widow in II Kings, to be penniless and then to lose her sons would have brought total devastation, but God protected her two most critical assets.

Notice, too, that He also multiplied her resources. God will give you ideas on how to take what you have and make it work. He multiplies what you have to make it work to meet the need. When the widow started, all she had was a pot of oil. Start where you are to take a step toward correcting your outgo.

Multiplication of resources was part of God's supernatural debt recovery plan for both widows. Whether it was "bake me a cake first," or "what do you have in the house?" God took what they had, multiplied their resources, and supernaturally made it work.

Every instance of supernatural instruction to the financially desperate qualifies as a poured-out idea from God. The ones we have looked at were both delivered by prophets, and we know that in the Old Testament the prophet stood for and spoke for God. He can also put poured-out ideas for your financial miracle in the mouths of other people.

Who Said That?

I've had situations where unbelievers spoke the word of the Lord without even knowing it. All of a sudden they would say something to me, and the Spirit of God would hit me. The person would have no idea God was using them to confirm His leading or instructions to me. We need to be open to all the different ways God can speak to us and communicate His poured-out ideas to deliver us out of financial bondage and into His perfect will. We don't want to be guilty of not paying attention and throwing aside a poured-out idea.

Once Again with Faith

Once we begin to act on His poured-out ideas and take whatever steps we can to correct our outgo, God is going to start making up the difference between what we need and what we have. He'll take up the slack supernaturally, closing the gap between what you can do and what needs to be done to get you out of debt. He may tell you to go back and do something that you failed at in the past, only this time will be different.

> ***...he (Jesus) stood by the lake of Gennesaret, And saw two ships standing by the lake: but the fishermen were gone out of them, and were washing their nets.... Launch out into the deep, and let down your nets for draught. And Simon answering said unto him, Master, we have toiled all the night, and have taken nothing: nevertheless at thy word I will let down the net. -Luke 5:1-2, 4***

The fishermen on the Sea of Galilee normally don't catch fish in the daytime, but this didn't matter to God. The disciples had a net-breaking, boat-sinking, mind-blowing catch because of one idea. God can certainly tell you to go back and do something that failed the first time you did it. I thought I was through building houses forever, yet God told me go back again and gave me the means to do it very successfully for a season.

The Bible shows us over and over again that Jesus was a comforter. In addition to bringing the comfort of healing where it was needed, He also knew how to bring the comfort of wealth to a needy situation. He knew where all the wealth was, and he knows today. In John 6, He knew how to supernaturally extend the resources of wealth to feed 5000 men with just five loaves and two fish. In Matthew 17, He knew where the gold coin was in the fish's mouth. Before He left the earth, He promised to send us another Comforter, the Holy Ghost, who would *take of His and show it unto us*

(John 16:15). Follow Him as He leads you out of debt and into abundance.

Conclusion

Putting it to Practice

Take Inventory of What You Have

Even if you think you can't give, or if you think you're so far in debt that you're beyond hope, take inventory of what you have. Quit worrying about what you don't have. God hates unused items and things going to waste. If you have something in your closet you have not worn or a microwave oven sitting in your garage, give it to somebody. If you've got an extra car, give it away or sell it.

The Lord pays attention to trivial things. I believe He appreciates us having a spirit of wanting to do *something* when we're bound by debt. Think of that little pot of oil or the little cake that triggered miracles of provision. Remember the unused donkey: The Lord had need of it, and He rode it through the streets of Jerusalem. You might have the biggest debt and the biggest mountain of financial difficulty in front of you, but even you can find something to give.

Keep Pouring

Keep pouring out. If all you have to give is your time, pour it out. Your time is worth something. Once my time was worth $6.50 an hour! Help clean your church. Use your skills to help someone else while you're looking for employment. In the example of the woman with the cruse of oil, her flow of provision didn't stop until she ran out of jars. The jars represent our opportunities to give.

The church I pastor owned 92 acres of virgin woods when God showed me we needed to begin pouring what we had into jars. Though we owned this land, we met in rented facilities for years waiting on provision for a building. What did we have in our house? Well, we had enough money to pay a clearing contractor. We poured out of what we had to get a large portion of our land cleared of underbrush.

The church began to have picnics on the land that had been cleared, and I would share the vision with our congregation and point out future landmarks of the building plan in my heart. These vision picnics also put the principle of possessing the land to work. Having cleared the land also meant keeping it mown, so we poured more oil in a jar labeled "church tractor." We poured some more oil into a contractor's jar and into an engineer's jar.

One day we got the estimate on the cost of the church building we have now, and the numbers just didn't work. Our property was worth about $1.2 million, and we still owed more than half a million. We could do no more. We had poured out all the money. Finally I said, "Lord, we've finished pouring out. Now what?"

A month later we got a call from the unsaved businessman who had financed the property for us. He said he needed a tax write-off. As it turned out, he wiped out our entire six-figure debt on the land, took it back, and replaced it with an 85-acre site worth almost $10 million. Now we owned the property outright! The new property was on a corner and had everything we wanted and more. Keep pouring!

Expect the Supernatural

If you take this revelation about ideas, concepts and insights back to your church, and they tithe and bring it with love and with a heart to see the gospel preached around the world—within less than a year, you will double, and even triple what you are able to give. -Dr. Oral Roberts

Expect the supernatural, and believe for the triple. Now that we have the right revelation, God can make it come back around for us, not only for the triple on tithes and offerings we *will* give, but also for the triple on what we have *already* given. It is hard to expect and believe for the supernatural when you are in debt and distressed, but God is waking up dead hope so our faith can triple up to reap His supernatural harvest. As my wife, Gladys, a cheerleader of the faith, has led our church in saying, "Triple up!"

Amazingly, the week before I flew to California to interview Dr. Oral Roberts, the Holy Ghost spoke to me and said, "Believe Me for triple." To be honest, I almost didn't want to share it with my church. *Triple* seemed huge—

certainly exceeding abundantly above all I could ask the people to join with me in believing. But because I knew it was according to His power and not mine, I did speak out and share what I'd heard with my congregation before I left for California.

Upon my return, my entire church watched the video of the interview and saw the look of shock on my face as Dr. Roberts boldly spoke "triple" into our future.

Your Abundance Is for God's Harvest

My prayer for you is that there will be no wasting of power for your release into abundance. The purpose of this overflow is for the harvest, and I want the revelation of *ideas, concepts and insights* to lift your expectation for a mighty transfer of wealth to come into your control. As Dr. Roberts wrote to me, this revelation is the very "guts of the gospel," and it is yours to receive now. Raise your hands and pray this prayer together with me from your heart:

Father, I bring my tithes and offerings to You with great love in my heart. I love You so much. I don't give because I have to. I give because I love You. This money is proof of my love. I give from a burning desire for Your Word to be preached all over the world. Father, I thank You for what I have learned through this book. My spirit has received fresh manna to strengthen me to reap the harvest for Your Kingdom. I choose to be a tither, and I repent for wrong expectations about Your tithe. Now, according to Malachi 3, I believe I receive ideas—so many ideas I cannot contain them. I am not going to receive someday, but I believe that I receive them now. I will be faithful to bring these ideas to fruition as You give me concepts. Thank You for wisdom and revelation. Show me how to work these things so a transfer of wealth will come under my control. Let me help pay for the harvest. Thank You for favor in the direction You want me to walk and for rebuking the devourer as You promised. Protect my assets— my family, my health, (List other assets as you desire.)—and I will give You all the glory and honor for the increase. I now rise up and reap in Jesus' name. Amen.

John Greiner

BIBLIOGRAPHY

[1] Barna Group (www.barna.org) "Americans Donate Billions to Charity, But Giving to Churches has Declined," April 25, 2005, pg. 2.

To order the *Wake-Up Call* on DVD during which Pastor John Greiner interviews Dr. Oral Roberts or for additional copies of this book and other ministry resource materials, please contact:

Glorious Way Church
11611 Champions Forest Drive
Houston, TX 77066
(281) 580-8806
www.gloriouswaychurch.org

To see a complete list of all **ADVANTAGE BOOKS™** visit our online bookstore at: www.advbookstore.com

or call our toll free order number at: 1-888-383-3110

Longwood, Florida, USA

"we bring dreams to life"™
www.advbookstore.com

Printed in the United States
53161LVS00002B/22-147